Deeper Than Belief

Kirk House Publishers

DEEPER THAN BELIEF

Why We Struggle to Trust God and Others
How Childhood Attachment Impacts Trust

MELINDA CATHEY

First printing, November 2025
First edition

Paperback ISBN: 978-1-968428-16-7
eBook ISBN: 978-1-968428-18-1
Hardcover ISBN: 978-1-968428-17-4

Library of Congress Control Number: Pending
Interior and Cover Design by Ann Aubitz

Scripture quotations are from the *New American Standard Bible (NASB)*.

Published by Kirk House Publishers
1250 E 115th Street
Burnsville, MN 55337
612-781-2815

To order, visit: kirkhousepublishers.com
Quantity discounts are available.

Dedicated to my children, Danielle Alyce, Micah John, and Breanne Noah, who have been my greatest teachers on all things pertaining to life and love, wounds and healing, grace and forgiveness. Being their mother has been my greatest joy in life.

And to Kai Jameson and Aria Grey, my grandchildren, who have taught me what it means to enter the Kingdom of God as a child and to understand on a much deeper level the peace, joy, and rest that comes with abiding trust.

ADVANCE PRAISE

We all need insight into why we are the way we are. Every one of us has been hurt, and every one of us has developed wrong thinking as a result. This wrong thinking impacts our relationships with God and others. It impacts our self-image. *Deeper than Belief* is a warm and easily understandable book that will help anyone who picks it up explore how your wounds have impacted you. And it goes beyond mere knowledge by offering many practical tools and Biblical insights to help bring healing.

~**Sandy McNickle,** a "wounded healer" who has been actively involved in journeying with others on the path of healing for 15 years.

Melinda's book is a long-awaited answer to the need in my own work, and many of my colleagues in Russia. Working with families we see the fundamental role trust plays in building strong close relationships. And how our learned way of "doing relationships" affects the way we see and relate to God. This book is a beautiful result of many years of Melinda's work with vulnerable people. It combines practical steps for counselors, pastors, small groups and individuals to understand our own story, build trusting relationships in families and communities, and learn to trust God more. As a counselor I look forward to using this book as a valuable resource. I recommend this book with deep hope that reading it we will see more of the love that our Heavenly Father has for us.

~**Galina Purcell,** psychologist, child development specialist and TBRI international practitioner.

In her book, *Deeper Than Belief,* Melinda Cathey does an excellent job of bringing spiritual truths to bear on our relational issues of trust. Her work is intensely practical, as she gets to the underlying reasons for our mistrust in God and those around us. Melinda's writing is born out of her personal story and years of counseling ministry experience. She is able to speak to the heart while giving a strong biblical rationale for a journey to healing and wholeness. It is a must-read for those eager to deepen their relationship of trust in the Father and help others do the same.

~**Dr. Cliff Wrener,** Lead Pastor, The Harbor Church, Hastings, MN; Missionary to China and Australia for 21 years, Bible teacher in Southeast Asia

ACKNOWLEDGMENTS

First and foremost, I am indebted to my friend and editor extraordinaire, Laura Greanias. Without her consistent encouragement, wise insights, profound questions, creativity, and professional excellence, this book would have never come to completion. I am deeply humbled and grateful for all the time and effort she put into this project. If this book helps anyone, it is in large measure due to Laura's work in bringing it forth. Thank you, Laura!

I also want to thank my dear husband, Mark, who endured my many tears and declarations of quitting this project with patience, grace, and humor. He held down the fort and added many more responsibilities to his already "too-full" plate to get me over the finish line. Thank you, Mark, for believing in me! Birthing this book also took the two of us. I'm so thankful to have you as my partner.

I am also thankful for my readers who took the time to plod through the first very rough draft and give feedback. Their encouragement was instrumental in giving me the motivation to finish. Thank you, Anya Gandy, Colleen Nunn, Melissa Thompson, Wendy Hawkins, Stephanie Wilkins, Galina Purcell, and Shellie Otto.

Lastly, I want to thank all those who have sat through my TBRI trainings in the past decade around the globe. It is because of your response to these trainings, and your persistent requests for me to write, that led me to begin this project in the first place. You all are my heroes. The work you do to care for orphans, foster children, and the most vulnerable among us inspires me beyond what you know. Your dedication to walk the path of your own healing in the process is beautiful. More than anything, I hope this book is helpful in your journey.

Foreword

In *Deeper Than Belief: Why We Struggle to Trust God and Others, How Childhood Attachment Impacts Trust* Melinda Cathey, with expertise and personal transparency, bridges the worlds of psychology, Christian faith, and personal healing, offering readers a profound exploration of the Attachment Cycle. Drawing from her deep experience, Melinda explains how the bonds we form—or fail to form—in our earliest years can profoundly shape our ability to trust not only people but also God in adulthood. If those foundational attachments were disrupted, she informs, it can lead to barriers that feel insurmountable, yet her message is one of hope. Healing is possible. Through lessons in Scripture she invites us to see God's goodness to humanity and reconsider His practical goodness in our personal lives.

I've had the privilege of knowing Melinda for nearly a decade, and her passion for this topic shines through in every page. As someone who's witnessed her transformative work in TBRI (Trust-Based Relational Intervention) training for the Christian camps we collaborate with, I can attest that her insights aren't just theoretical—they're inspired, born from a genuine calling to help others rebuild what was broken. Melinda's approach is compassionate, biblically grounded, and practical, making complex concepts accessible while inviting readers to reflect on their own stories.

This book isn't just a read; it's a roadmap to deeper connections and spiritual intimacy. Whether you're struggling with trust issues or simply seeking to understand them better, *Deeper Than Belief* will inspire you to pursue the attachments that lead to true fulfillment, for yourself, your family and most importantly, your relationship with God. Highly recommended!"

~**Bryan C. Johnson**—Founder and Executive Director of Psalm68five Ministries, A ministry to the fatherless. Past President BC Johnson Associates, Petroleum Engineering

TABLE OF CONTENTS

	Introduction	15
SECTION 1	ATTACHMENT AND TRUST IN GOD AND OTHERS	25
Chapter 1	To Trust or Not to Trust. Where It All Starts.	27
	Understanding the Attachment Cycle	27
	The Attachment Cycle teaches us about dependence	36
	The Attachment Cycle teaches us about using our voice and prayer	40
	The Attachment Cycle teaches us about the names and character of God	41
Chapter 2	Where It All Went Wrong	49
	Adam and Eve (Genesis 2-4)	49
	Pride vs. trust	54
	Rebellion vs. trust	56
	Connection and trust	57
Chapter 3	How Broken Trust Became Generational Dysfunction	67

Insecure attachment styles and how they impact relationships with God and others   65

Avoidant Attachment   70

Ambivalent Attachment   74

Disorganized Attachment   76

More about the importance of "Voice"   80

Chapter summary: The essence of trust   83

SECTION 2   CORRECTIVE EXPERIENCES FROM GOD TO REGAIN TRUST   91

Chapter 4   Learning the Character of God Through Experiences   93

Abraham and Israel: Trusting God's provision, power, and intentions   96

Common obstacles to trusting the Lord   101

Where do you start if you've never started or if you have great difficulty trusting the Lord   127

Chapter 5   Learning the Personal Nature of God Through Experiences   137

I know you, I see you   137

SECTION 3   HEALING WITH HUMANITY   149

Chapter 6   Developing Earned Security and Learning to Trust Others   151

Chapter 7   Conclusion: The Journey   183

About the Author   189

INTRODUCTION

My life has been characterized by deep internal struggle. I'm sure this is what ultimately led me into the field of psychology and caused me to become a therapist. As someone once said, "Research really should be called 'Me-search.'"

All of my study has had the dual purpose of better understanding myself as well as others. I have struggled to understand myself: why I think, feel, and respond the way I do. I have wrestled with the tension between a pervading sense of deep aloneness and my inability to do the things I know would be helpful to mitigate this. I have come to understand that the reason is rooted in my core inability to trust others to be there for me in significant ways.

I did not come to this conclusion without reason. It has been my lived experience. Nevertheless, it creates a vicious cycle of internal isolation I long to break.

Since my early childhood, Jesus has been my best friend. Yet even with Him, there has been significant wrestling. I grew up in the church but lived a double life. Even as a little girl, I was drawn to Jesus and the Scriptures, but I could not understand how to live what the Scriptures taught, and I did not know anyone who actually lived that way. Church seemed to give me a template of guidelines by which to order my life, yet the heart of the Father behind these guidelines was never explained. I was introduced to knowledge about Jesus. His life, death, and resurrection moved me. But I thought He was distant and His promises were only for the future, for the "by and by."

Nevertheless, His Spirit kept drawing me and I started seriously reading Scripture on my own in middle school. The result was increasing tension between His Spirit and my flesh that reached an unbearable point by the end of my freshman year in college. I could no longer live this double life. I had to choose one way or the other.

A deeply personal "Damascus road" experience, like that of Paul, led me to prostrate myself on the floor of the chapel at my university. I had reached the end of myself and chose to give the rest of my life to follow Jesus, though I had no idea how to do that. The abrupt change in my lifestyle led to the separation of a lot of friendships. I entered a period of deep loneliness and confusion, yet I knew there was no turning back. All I could do was read Scripture, pray as best I knew how, and go to classes.

In the ensuing months and years, the Lord met me in profound ways. He brought many believers into my life who began to teach me how to read the Scriptures and live them. Jesus was no longer only a historical person, but He became real and present to me in the moment. I learned to hear His voice and see His leading in my life and circumstances. I began to experience His comfort and love in ways I never knew possible.

When I went to college, I had no idea what I wanted to do, but I knew it would be something in science. I considered archeology, zoology, botany, biology, and forensic chemistry. I finally landed on a double major in psychology and biology. At this time, I was growing in my knowledge of both science and the Scriptures. There was no problem or disconnect for me in doing so. My father was a dentist who also loved science and the Scriptures. He taught me to never be afraid to ask questions in either area, firmly believing that "the truth will always win out."

Science informed my faith, and my faith informed my study of science. However, my desire to integrate the two was met with shocking intolerance from both sides. I was kicked out of both a biology and psychology class for suggesting that humanity possessed a spiritual component as well as physical.

Then, after college, I got my first job working for a large Christian campus ministry. I was leading a Bible study with several girls. In a single week, one girl found out her parents were divorcing, another one confessed she was struggling with alcohol addiction and homosexuality, and a third one's mother was killed in a car accident. I felt lost in how to help them in their extreme individual pain. This led to my desire to pursue graduate school in counseling psychology. I was publicly shamed by the leadership for deciding to "punt ministry for the sake of psychology." Their argument was that memorizing Bible verses was sufficient for such issues.

I landed at Trinity Evangelical Divinity School, where I received my Master of Arts in Counseling Psychology with a minor in biblical studies. I worked in a community mental health setting, in a large mega-church counseling center, and in private practice before moving as a missionary to St. Petersburg, Russia. I was exposed to close to 90% of the diagnoses in the Diagnostic and Statistical Manual and worked very hard to apply an integrated model of good psychology and biblical principles to my clients.

In 1992, I moved to St. Petersburg with my husband, Mark, and our 14-month-old daughter. Mark was to lead a team of church planters in the newly opened Russia. I spent the first year trying to find enough daily food for our family to survive, learn the language, and help our daughter, Danielle, and myself assimilate to the culture. As the years went on, I had two more children, learned the language, and fell in love with the culture.

I was so moved by the level of trauma. This was not the Russia I had learned about in my history classes. The vastness of the brokenness throughout the whole culture was overwhelming. There was no apparent functioning institution or societal infrastructure. Family, church, government, economy, education—all in shambles. And I learned that the people had been oppressed for a very long thousand-year history, not just the recent 70-year Communist regime. I had a deep desire to use my counseling experience to help but had no clue how.

One day, the Lord brought a 19-year-old orphan, Alex Krutov, to our apartment door. His story is detailed in his book *Infinitely More*. Alex came to our apartment looking for a job. He had recently aged out of the orphanage system and had learned some cooking skills that he was hoping I could use. I was struck by how bad he looked. Several of his teeth were rotting, and he was extremely thin with his ribs protruding through his white T-shirt. That is all he was wearing on this very cold November day in Russia. I didn't need a cook but invited him in for lunch.

Alex became a part of our family and over time his story unfolded. I found out he had spent his whole life in the orphanage system. At age 13, Alex became a believer through some visiting U.S. missionaries and was currently leading Bible studies in several orphanages. I began to go with him.

Hanging out with the orphans, I began to ask them about their dreams and plans. I'll never forget when one young man looked at me and said, "Only Americans can dream. I'm just trying to get through today and tomorrow." The more I got involved, the more the statistics made sense. At that time, we learned that only 5% of the orphans would make it into some kind of successful adulthood. The remainder ended up in jail, criminal activity, homeless or dead within five years of leaving the orphanage. Russian society had too many other problems to try to tackle this issue. In addition, most Russians had a warped sense of fate or karma that led a large part of the population to believe that the status of orphan was somehow their own fault.

In a very long story that is worthy of its own book, the Lord directed me and Alex to dream an audacious dream about helping this orphan population that was aging out of the system around 16 or 17 years old. We began The Harbor to basically reparent these orphans and give them everything they needed to be able to live a successful independent adult life: education, life skills, counseling, Bible studies, and a family life experience.

Walking with these precious young adults as they navigate their lives and try to overcome all the trauma and strikes against them has been a beautiful and daunting journey for me. It has stretched me both personally and professionally, bringing me to the end of myself on many occasions.

Simultaneously, I had many issues in my own life to navigate. Raising three children in Russia in the 1990s and early 2000s was fraught with all kinds of danger and trauma, which they carry to this day. I lost both parents in 1998 in a month's span. My mother was killed in a car accident. My father died from a work-related lung disease. Four years later, my 18-year-old nephew was killed in a car accident three weeks after he graduated from high school. Betrayals from ministry partners, relational conflicts, financial burdens, and health issues were happening in my world in addition to working with the orphans.

Life was heavy. Most Christian input I was exposed to at the time seemed incredibly superficial and completely unsatisfying for my reality. The pat answers just made me angry. I had come to know the Jesus who meets people in the messy places of their lives, who sits with them, comforts them, and teaches them while they are still in darkness. I longed to know Him more and do a better job of showing Him to others in their brokenness.

This book is a compilation of what the Lord has revealed to me in my personal journey of following Him and having to face my own wounds that have plagued and limited me. Most of these insights have come through my studies of Trust Based Relational Intervention (TBRI) and all the related disciplines (developmental psychology, developmental trauma, attachment theory, interpersonal neurobiology, mindfulness, and somatic therapy).

This is not meant to be a deep dive into theology or attachment psychology. Thus, several theological and attachment concepts are not fully developed here. I am picking and choosing to make specific points. As I have shared these insights with others, they have told me how powerfully transformative they have been. My hope is that you will also find that to be true.

When I began studying attachment theory about 10 years ago, I had already been a mental health counselor for 25 years and the director of our residential program in Russia for 15 years. Despite our overall success at The Harbor, I was frustrated with our inability to reach about 10% of the kids' hearts. What were we missing? Neither our Russian psychologist nor I were able to come up with any answers. The short version of a long story is that I met the co-founders of TBRI, Drs. Karyn Purvis and David Cross, and had the great privilege of studying under them before Dr. Purvis' untimely death.

What started as continuing education for my professional work has turned into life transformation in deep and surprising ways. Learning attachment theory helped heal deep personal wounds more than any other therapy or education I received in the previous 25 years. It transformed the way I read the Word of God and understood the Gospel. It changed the way I related to God and people and shared the Good News. I now train other missionaries, programs, and organizations in this trauma-informed intervention all over the globe.

As I see others respond the same way I did, I understand that all true science simply reveals the character of God and His unchangeable design for His creation. When we live in alignment with His design, there is healing and wholeness. When we live contrary to His design, there is brokenness and all kinds of dysfunctions.

Clearly, the Lord's design in creation is so exhaustive that all the current research in the world has not come close to fully explaining it. We get bits and pieces. In this book, I'm attempting to pull out one thread, the one I believe is the most important: the thread of trust. In our current world, trust is a hard commodity to come by, whether in governments, families, social institutions, employers, or other nations. I think this concept needs to be revisited and more deeply understood, especially by the Church.

The world is desperate for a Church that has ingested Jesus—not just knowledge about Him. It can be far too easy to give mental assent to doctrine and miss Him entirely. We do well to heed James' warning, "You say you have faith because you believe there is a God. Good for you! Even the demons believe that" (James 2:19, my paraphrase).

True faith is deeper than belief. True faith goes beyond the words we say we believe. It captures our heart and transforms our whole being. The true essence of faith is trust, the ability to lay our heads on Jesus' chest in the boat and take a nap with Him as the storm is raging. This is His longing for us as He urges us to *not* be a people who honors Him with their lips only and whose hearts are far from Him (Matthew 15:8-9).

Nothing ultimately good can happen without trust. Given that, it sure would be nice if we were simply born with this ability. But, alas, we are not. Rather, trust is something you learn—or don't. How does this happen?

SECTION 1
ATTACHMENT AND TRUST IN GOD AND OTHERS

TO TRUST OR NOT TO TRUST
WHERE IT ALL STARTS

Understanding the Attachment Cycle

When you really think about it, your ability to trust (or not) is foundational to how you live and love. Do you trust others to listen to you, take care of you, protect you, really have your back when all the chips are stacked against you? Do you trust that people will respond positively to your requests for your needs and/or boundaries? If so, you will easily enter into relationships, friendships, and romantic relationships with an openness and expectation of a mutual give and take. If not, you will be defensive, feeling a need to take care of yourself and be on the lookout for how others are going to take advantage of you.

The same is true with employers, sports teams, or larger institutions. Without trust, it is impossible to have a sense of loyalty. You will default to a completely under-standable "dog eat dog" position. If you don't know that the employer, coach, or government has your back, then you are on your own. In any given situation when it comes to the inevitable clash of what's best for you versus what's best for the "company," you will choose what's best for you. How else will you survive?

I submit to you that our ability to trust (or not) and who we trust are the most important drivers of how we live and the greatest predictors of our overall satisfaction in life. Furthermore, I think that what the Lord wants, what He requires from us as human beings, more than anything else is TRUST. You might say, "No, He wants us to love Him with all our heart, soul, mind, and strength." This is not possible without TRUST. **Trust is the antecedent for love**. You do not and will not love someone you cannot trust. Without trust, you will never give them your heart.

God longs for us to trust Him so that we will obey Him and walk with Him and watch His goodness flow over and through our lives, and so we can give testimony to the world about how good, kind, loving, faithful, merciful, and beautiful He is.

Make no mistake. What is up for debate in the heavenlies is God's goodness. Is He good? Is He worthy of trust? This is the question Satan has posed to humanity (and I believe to the angels) from the very beginning. Everything rests on how we answer this. And God tells us we cannot come to Him unless we believe He is God and He is good (Hebrews 11:6). That means we need to trust Him.

TRUST is not a completely equivalent synonym for BELIEF. Our English Bible uses the words trust and belief interchangeably. There is a very important difference. Belief is, "Do I think you are telling me the truth?" Trust goes beyond this. Trust involves a relational component. It is the result of KNOWING the person by having experiences with them. Can I rely on you? Are you good? Are you for me? **It is possible for me to believe you and yet not trust you**. For example, you might tell me some gossip that I know is true. I believe you. But I certainly will not trust you with my secrets. This is the position of demons who certainly DO believe God but certainly DO NOT trust Him (James 2:19).

On the other hand, if I trust you, I will also believe you. I will not trust you if I think you are a liar. Trust implies a knowing of the person, their character, and their intentions toward you. And knowing that these flow from a heart of goodness and love.

Belief does not equal trust.

Belief ≠ Trust

Trust = Knowing a person (their character, intentions, reliability, goodness) + Belief (are they telling the truth)

Trust = Knowing + Belief

TRUST is what God is getting at in Isaiah 43:10. He chose us to **know and understand Him** through His great works. It is His great works for and among His people that allow them to see His character. On the basis of these works of His, we are to come to see, understand, know, and trust that He is the only God and Savior, and that He is good. "Let him who boasts boast in this, that he **knows and understands Me**" (Jeremiah 9:24). He also says, "My people are foolish. They do not know Me. They are stupid children and have no understanding of Me" (Jeremiah 4:22). He wants us to know Him as a good Father so that we may trust Him as such (Jeremiah 3:19, Romans 8:15, Matthew 6:9).

This minuscule distinction is critical for us to understand. It is easy to confuse the two and deceive ourselves. To do a reality check, I now substitute the word trust for belief in any passage of Scripture I'm studying and then pay attention to my body. I encourage you to try it. Our bodies respond to what we really think and believe. We can fool our minds, but we cannot fool our bodies. If I truly trust the Lord with any given promise, the result will be **peace**, **hope**, and **joy**. My body will tell me if this is my true state or not.

While I was wrestling in prayer for months over a situation, I had a debate with the Lord about this. He said to me, "You don't trust me." "Yes, I do," I replied, and I began to list off a series of Bible verses that I had memorized and given mental assent to. "Well then, why are you anxious? Why are you not sleeping? Why is your stomach in knots, your heart racing, and you're not able to focus? Why is your mind constantly preoccupied with worries about the future?" Ouch! Trust results in rest. We are confident in a secure relationship. It is "being still and knowing that He is God" (Psalm 46:10).

Getting to this place of trust with the Lord is easier for some than others. It's harder for those who have experienced more suffering and broken relationships. These are the brothers and sisters who we are told to "strengthen their hands which are weak and their knees which are feeble, to help make their paths straight so that their limbs which are lame will be healed and not put out of joint" (Hebrews 12:12-13).

When the Church does not understand the difference between trust and belief or how they develop, it's easy to just focus on the behaviors of others. Our behaviors are merely the expressions of whom we truly trust. If we don't understand this and simply teach "You need to obey," we miss the heart, the driving force behind the obedience or the lack thereof. The recipients of this teaching feel terribly misunderstood, unloved, and rejected. The result is either pushing down your true heart and striving or walking away in anger with "church wounds." Neither is what the Lord wants.

Understanding obstacles in our ability to trust the Lord is the key to unlocking what keeps us (and others) stuck. Unraveling this is not merely a cognitive exercise but requires soul work.

It's not lost on the Lord that He is Spirit, and we are flesh. He understands the inherent difficulty we have in trusting an invisible God. So He gives us physical realities by which we are meant to understand the invisible spiritual realm. Romans 1:19-20 tells us that the Father's invisible attributes, eternal power, and divine nature have been made visible to us in what He created. This includes, but is not limited to, what we typically think of as "the creation", such as the mountains and the trees. The infinite Creator uses so many more physical realities to give us insights into who He is. If only we had eyes to see! Through my studies on the Attachment Cycle, I have come to believe that it is one such beautiful metaphor, a physical reality teaching a much deeper spiritual truth.

The Attachment Cycle is the way we learn as infants to understand who we are, what the world is like, strategies for how to develop relationships, and whether or not to trust. We learn this through our relationship with our primary caregiver, whether parent, foster parent, grandparent, nanny, etc. The way in which they see us and meet our needs literally becomes wired into our brains by the time we are around 12 months old.

It's very much like programming software. The software we have, our specific attachment style, remains consistent throughout our lifespan and across different types of relationships. This means that what we learn in our infancy about trust and how to do relationships translates into how we do friendships, romantic relationships, and work relationships in our adulthood. It becomes the lens through which we see and interpret our reality. Without awareness and intentional change, our understanding of trust and relationships remains fixed. (Spoiler alert: Thankfully, we are able to heal and change our software!)

As infants, we come into the world completely dependent upon our primary caregiver to keep us alive. We have no clue what we need to survive nor the ability to provide it for ourselves. We're helpless. The only thing we can do is cry in response to our body sending stress signals to our brain whenever it senses a need; hunger, fear, boredom, having a dirty diaper, being tired, being too hot or too cold, etc. As infants, we have seemingly endless needs. We cry a lot! Over and over we cry, and our caregiver responds. **How** our caregiver responds is the key.

Ideally, our primary caregiver will pay attention to our cry and meet our needs **adequately**, **predictably**, and **with emotional nurturing**. All three aspects of care are necessary for the development of a healthy brain, body, soul and identity. The absence of any of these will result in significant deficits in one or more areas of development (which is further explained in Chapter 3). Adequately means you were given enough food, appropriate types of clothing, and shelter. It means your caregiver knew how to hold you properly so that you felt strongly supported but not hurt, it also means your needs were met quickly and that you were not left in a state of distress for hours or days. Predictably means you could count on your needs being met when you cried. You were not left wondering, "Is my caregiver coming or not? Am I going to get my needs met or not?" Emotionally nurturing means your caregiver attends to your emotional state as well as your physical need. Your soul is being seen and attended too as well as your body and behaviors.

If this happens, you as the infant wire profound messages into your brain. Through your primary caregiver's behavior, you understand at a core soul level the messages of **Felt-Safety**. Your caregiver is communicating:

- I see you
- I hear you
- I will not abandon you or leave you alone
- I will comfort you
- I will meet your needs
- I will protect you
- I will delight in you

As a result of these messages, the infant you further wires messages about your identity, the world, and how to do relationships:

- I am loved, valued, and worthy of care and attention.
- My voice matters: I can cry and get my needs met.
- The world is safe, a good place; I can relax in it.
- Others can be trusted.

Again, understand that all these messages become encoded neurologically in a baby's brain in the subconscious, preverbal, limbic region. The infant you has no conscious words or thoughts at this point. This is all the background messaging, the infrastructure of our brain and mind, the default position of our souls. Our brains are designed to be efficient, so we don't have to learn the same things over and over again every day. Once programmed, the software just runs. Thus, **our past experiences "prime" our brains about how to interpret the present and anticipate the future.** They are like a pair of lenses through which we see and understand the world.

If this is your software, you have what is called a **Secure Attachment** style and you are set up for good outcomes. It's relatively easy for you to enter into relationships in a way where you can give nurture, receive nurture, adequately negotiate your needs, and have a secure and stable sense of identity. Of course, things can happen later in life to change this trajectory, but that's a matter for another chapter.

The Attachment Cycle teaches us about dependence

The Father wants us to relate to Him just like an infant who is completely dependent and fully trusting. He wants us to realize we are helpless in the ultimate things of life and to cry to Him for these things. If you look again at Scripture with this filter, you'll begin to see how often the Lord's frustration with His children is due to their lack of trusting Him to take care of them! The result is they do not cry out to Him and ask for their needs. We have not because we ask not (James 4:2). Nor do they share their anxieties with Him "Cast all your anxiety upon Him, because He cares for you" (1 Peter 5:7). Innocence, humility, dependence—these are the hallmarks of being a child. These are the character qualities required for those who enter the Kingdom of God.

My grandchildren, still toddlers, have not yet reached the age where they think they can meet their own needs. It is beautiful to behold. When my grandson needs help fixing one of his toys, he says, "Let's go to Daddy. He'll fix it." Or as he recently told me, "We can't do that. Mommy said no." When my granddaughter is tired or hungry, she will crawl into my daughter's lap. She does not yet have the words to tell Mommy what she needs, but she implicitly knows if she gets to Mommy, her needs will be met. Somehow, Mommy figures this out.

This is what the Lord meant when He commanded us to become like children. "Truly I say to you, unless you are converted and become like children, you shall not enter the Kingdom of heaven" (Matthew 18:3). Children understand their dependence without question and do not fight it. It just is. But the older we get, the harder it is to embrace the reality of our dependence on God and others. It feels weak and vulnerable. Thus, we constantly try to free ourselves from these shackles and become independent. In doing so, we fight against reality and against our design—to our peril.

God designed us as dependent beings on purpose and with a purpose. First, our dependence is a reflection of being created in His Triune image, the community of three perfectly interdependent beings. It is also the nature of being a creature instead of the Creator. Like a child, we do not know what we need for abundant life, nor do we have the ability to provide it for ourselves in any ultimate sense.

Dependence is beautiful. It allows for developing trust. **You have to be dependent on another to learn whether or not you can trust them.** How else will you know if they are reliable? When trust is earned, then there is a desire to connect and attach to another. Love is born. Look back at the previous sentence, "when trust is earned." Trust must be earned. This is astounding to me. The Lord Himself says in His Word, "faith without works is useless" (James 2:14-26). He understands it's easy to say something, but to be trusted, what you say needs to be backed up with actions. **Our dependence on God gives Him the ability to prove His faithfulness and trustworthiness.** He put Himself in this position of vulnerability. Is He really willing and able to meet all of our needs? All of His promises and mighty works are intended to prove His character and win the hearts and trust of His children (Matthew 7:11, Malachi 3:10).

Dependence creates the atmosphere for giving and receiving. I need you, and you need me. Without dependence, we will choose to go the "lone ranger" path and suffer the consequences of isolation and loneliness. This is why more affluent communities have higher rates of depression than poorer communities. We are designed to need each other and God. Fighting against my dependence on God and others always leads to fear, anxiety, and attempts to control my reality.

Understanding the purpose and fruits of dependence helps me embrace it with those who have proven to be trustworthy. To the degree I do, I will live in peace.

Dependence, trust, attachment, and love are inextricably linked. You cannot separate them.

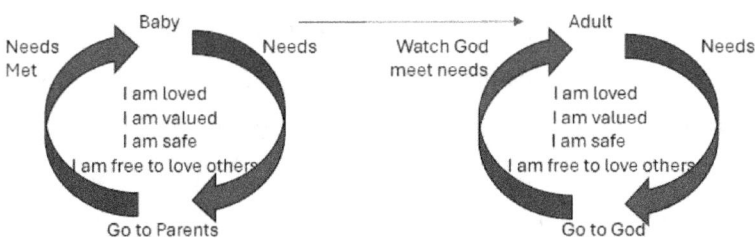

If our needs are not met as babies, we will not grow up feeling loved, valued, and safe. And we must feel those things in order to love others. If we don't, we will spend our time in self-protection and self-promotion to try to get our needs met by ourselves.

This is the challenge Jesus is presenting us in His teaching in Matthew 6. He beckons us to trust Him to take care of us—not just our spiritual salvation someday in heaven, but here and now. He's saying, "Depend on Me for your physical needs of money, food, shelter, and clothing just like a baby and watch me provide." This is challenging. But if we get it, we will live lives of peace and fullness, being free to love others, resting in Him, and living the destiny He intends for us. How else can we learn that He is good and we can trust Him without becoming dependent and experiencing Him faithfully meeting our needs?

The Attachment Cycle teaches us about using our voice and prayer

The Attachment Cycle shows us other aspects of God's character. We see that when the baby has needs, the only power he has is his ability to cry. This is the baby's voice, and it's powerful. A baby's cry changes the heart rate and body chemistry of the mother. It creates stress within her, arousing her to attend to her baby and meet his needs. This is intended to be instructive to us regarding our Heavenly Father as well. He is the perfect parent. He will not abandon us (Isaiah 49:15-16). He will listen to our cries when we call upon Him (Matt 7:7-11).

Our voice was given to us as a powerful tool. He means for us to use it for good. Jesus' voice speaks things into being. The prophets and disciples did too. Through their voices, they moved things in the heavenlies, stopped the rain, brought about leadership changes in Israel and world governments, healed blind eyes, raised the dead, and many other things. The very first command to Adam was God telling him to use his voice and name the animals. "We will call them whatever you call them" (Genesis 2:19, my paraphrase).

So often we don't trust the Lord because we don't see Him working. The problem is we quit asking and cease using our voices (Isaiah 43:22, James 4:2). If we look at the Attachment Cycle and see how a baby asks for his needs and the parent responds, it gives us courage to cry to our Father in similar fashion. We have a physical model for understanding the parables of Jesus about relentless prayer (Luke 11:5-18, Luke 18:1-8).

The Attachment Cycle teaches us about the names and character of God
Looking back at the messages of **Felt-Safety** the infant receives from an attuned caregiver, we can see they are actually the names of God! This is who He reveals Himself to be throughout Scripture.

- I see you: The God who sees. While running away from her abusive master, Hagar meets the Lord in the wilderness in a tender and instructive way, leading her out of her predicament. She declares, "You are a God who sees" (Genesis 16:13).

- I hear you: The God who hears (Psalm 4:3)
- I will meet all your needs: The God who provides (Matthew 6:33)
- I will protect you: The God who protects us (Psalm 4:8, Psalm 121)
- I will be with you: The God who does not abandon you (John 14:18, Matthew 28:20)
- I will comfort you: The God of comfort (Psalm 86:17)
- I will delight in you: The God who delights in you (Zephaniah 3:17)

There are many other verses for each aspect of God's character revealed to us through this Attachment Cycle. It bears repeating. God designed the Attachment Cycle as the way babies were to get their needs met, learn how to trust and do relationships, and understand their identity. It is also a metaphor for how He wants us to relate to Him. He desires that we understand our complete dependence on Him in matters of life and death, that we cry to Him, and that we **experience** Him meeting our needs. As we experience His great works toward us, we learn about His character and that He can be trusted. We learn our identity in Him as His beloved children. We feel loved, protected, valued, and safe. In His perfect love, all fear is cast out (1 John 4:18). It is only natural to love Him back.

As we all know, the design quickly went amok. What happened?

Chapter 1 Meditations

1. Which of the messages of a Secure Attachment do you experience with friends and significant others? Which ones do you struggle with? Do you experience them telling you through their words and actions …
   - I see you
   - I hear you
   - I will not abandon you or leave you alone
   - I will comfort you
   - I will meet your needs
   - I will protect you
   - I will delight in you

2. Which of the messages of a Secure Attachment are easy for you to experience with the Lord? Not easy?
   - I see you
   - I hear you
   - I will not abandon you or leave you alone
   - I will comfort you
   - I will meet your needs
   - I will protect you
   - I will delight in you

- Which Person of the Trinity (Father, Son, or Holy Spirit) do you find easiest to trust? Hardest to trust? Why might that be?

3. Can you remember specific examples of how/when your primary caregiver gave you these messages through their words or actions?
   - I see you
   - I hear you
   - I will not abandon you or leave you alone
   - I will comfort you
   - I will meet your needs
   - I will protect you
   - I will delight in you
   - How did they relate to you in conflict? Rejecting? Constructively? Was there a time of repairing the relationship when the conflict was over?
   - If these were not the messages you received, what messages did you receive?

Note: It's not unusual to have difficulty remembering our childhood. Practice trying to remember and memories begin to surface. You can also ask older siblings or relatives.

4. Do you exhibit the four characteristics of a Secure Attachment style?
   - An ability to both give and receive nurture
   - An ability to use my voice
   - An ability to negotiate my needs
   - A stable sense of my own identity, able to disagree with others without losing myself or trying to control, manipulate, or change them. I can allow others to be separate.

Chapter 1 References

1. Trust-Based Relational Intervention® from the original Participants Workbooks: *TBRI® Introduction and Overview, TBRI® Connecting Principles, TBRI® Empowering Principles*, and *TBRI® Correcting Principles*, by Purvis, K.; Cross, D.R.; Hurst, J.R.; Milton, H. (2013)
2. *The Power of Showing Up*, by Daniel J. Siegel, M.D., and Tina Payne Bryson, Ph.D. (2021)
3. *The Whole-Brain Child*, by Daniel J. Siegel, M.D., and Tina Payne Bryson, Ph.D. (2012)
4. *Affect Regulation and the Origin of the Self*, first edition, by Allan N. Schore, Ph.D. (2015)
5. *The Brain That Changes Itself*, by Norman Doidge, M.D. (2007)
6. *The Developing Mind*, by Daniel J. Siegel, M.D. (1999)
7. The Strange Situation experiment, by Mary Ainsworth, Ph.D., YouTube
8. The Still Face experiment, by Edward Tronick, Ph.D., YouTube
9. Rhesus monkey studies, by Harry Harlow, Ph.D., YouTube

WHERE IT ALL WENT WRONG

Adam and Eve (Genesis 2-4)

If trust is the foundation of how we live and love, if it is the necessary component for attaching to God and others, and if you were the enemy of God and humanity, wouldn't you go after destroying this? In destroying the ability to trust, you can destroy one's relationship with oneself, others, and God. You will succeed in robbing humanity of all God intended for them.

God's intention for His children to live in peace and joy is replaced with them living in **anger, fear**, and **sadness**. His desire for them to receive His abundant life is replaced with His children living lives of striving through **self promotion, self protection,** and **control.** God's design for community is replaced with **isolation.** It's a brilliant strategy that the enemy unfolded with our first ancestors and has had ripple effects down through the generations. The strategy has not changed one bit, and each successive generation continues to "bite the apple." Let's take a look at the story of Adam and Eve.

Think about how you interpret this story. What are the assumptions—likely subconscious—that you've made about God and humanity here? It's not unusual when we look at the story of Adam and Eve to think of sin and rebellion. Eve **disobeyed** God. She **sinned** and encouraged Adam to sin as well. God responded with **righteous judgment** and **punishment.** Adam and Eve "missed the mark," and the consequence or cost of their sin was death. The story of our original sin becomes about rebellion and lack of obedience. It **becomes about our behavior**. This is the story most of us understand.

While all of this is technically correct, I have come to wonder if it misses the whole point of the story and is responsible for much of our misunderstanding of who the Father really is. In fact, I think this reading of the story often feeds into the very lie the enemy used to lead Eve astray.

In this rendition of the story, God is a strict disciplinarian. He responds to disobedience with swift and harsh punishment. The punishment is so severe, He casts them away from His presence. It is the very first "time out."

This is a scary God. If you don't get it right or are feeling a bit defiant, He will abandon you. This does not highlight His goodness or His love but rather His need to be feared. Who wants to come near to a God like that? And yet we must or else we will go to hell. Yikes.

We end up coming to Him trembling like Dorothy in *The Wizard of Oz* coming to face the wizard. This God is hard to give our hearts to. This is not at all the picture Jesus paints of His Father. **What if the story is not so much about our behavior but more about our heart? What if it is about who, what, and why we choose to trust and the result of that choice?**

What was Eve's sin? Disobeying a command of the Lord. Why did she do that? Because she ceased trusting Him! I think this is the point of the story. How did this happen? Let's take a closer look.

The enemy starts his dialogue with Eve by sowing doubt: "Did God really say ... you cannot eat from any tree in the garden?" Eve responds correctly, "No, He said ... we can eat from any tree but the one in the middle or we will die." Then Satan lays the hammer down: "You will not die!"

Think about this. His response to the Word of God is, "God is a liar!" His further explanation tells Eve, "God is not good. He's jealous. He doesn't want to share His power and glory with you. He's holding out on you. He doesn't want to give you what's best. That tree in the middle is what's best, and He doesn't want you to have it because you will become like Him. You will be a competitor to Him."

This is the enemy's strategy: First he **sows doubt about God's Word** (what did He really say). Then he **sows doubt about God's character** (He is a liar) **and His intentions** toward us (unloving and selfish). Then he **redefines God's word** (life and death) and **reinterprets our "objective circumstances"** (the tree, the apple) in a way that feeds our pride and awakens rebellion. After all that, he **challenges Eve to "look again."** "Look at it!" Now what does she see? It's no longer something that will harm her, but it "looks good and desirable to make her wise." **What we see is determined by what we hear.** His strategy has not changed.

Eve faces the ultimate choice. Who is she going to trust? She has been presented with two different and opposing stories of reality: God is good, God is not good. The tree is good for you, the tree is harmful for you. You will live, you will die. Eat it, don't eat it.

Two ways to "see" and "understand" the circumstances before her. She has to choose. As we all know, she ends up making the fatal choice to believe the lie.

Why? Why would she trust Satan? In his redefining her reality (the tree and apple), he certainly tempts her pride by giving her the false promise she could be her own god. Satan is telling her she doesn't need to be dependent on God. Though certainly appealing, I don't think this was enough to cause Eve to make the choice she did.

Again, I turn to my grandson. Last week I was encouraging him to eat his dinner so that he could grow big and become like daddy. His response was precious and powerful. "I don't want to become big. I like being little." He is enjoying the fruits of a secure childhood. He trusts his mommy and daddy. He loves being dependent and getting to play all day while they have to worry about how to care for him. Many of us can remember sharing this same sentiment.

I believe the root cause of Eve's choice was when Satan convinced her that God was not good. So she ceased trusting Him and what He had told her. *We only trust one we think is good.* We will never choose to trust one we think is unreliable, unloving, uncaring, or selfish. We certainly will not give them our hearts or willingly submit to and obey them! This process is mostly subconscious, but it's happening all the time. We need to learn to pay attention to all the voices in our heads telling us who to believe and defining right, wrong, and reality for us. We need to consider who's telling us these things. Are they good? Are they for us? Are they telling us the truth? How do we know?

How could Eve have known the character of God? What proof had He given her? The first two chapters of

Genesis give us some clues. The Lord had provided everything she needed in life. She was in want of nothing. Eve lived in perfect harmony with all of creation and non-conflictual intimacy with God and her husband. Perhaps she took all this for granted. After all, it was all she had known. Maybe she did not attribute all these blessings to God. Somehow, she missed the clear signs of His goodness.

More than understanding this story as a warning of rebellion, I think it's a story about the character of God and who we are going to trust with our lives. The two are inseparable. Is He good? Is He truthful? Is He the one who gets to define reality (the tree, the apple, life, and death) or not? The warning is about what happens when we choose not to trust God.

Pride vs. trust

Pride is a false assessment of reality that impedes our ability to trust. I think it's fair to say that a little child does not have pride. Pride is saying, "I do it myself. I don't need you. I can be my own boss." Instinctually, little children know they can't take care of themselves. They're completely fine depending on their parents, especially if their parents are good and kind. It's easy for the child to trust their parents.

But something happens around ages 2 and 3. That feisty will begins to surface. The once humble and docile child experiences some degree of independence—and it's addictive. Without nurturing structure placed on this budding independence, it will become a self-destructive monster. We all know this to be true.

In childhood, this pride or arrogance comes from a false sense of what they can do. Having mastered dressing themselves, they believe they can walk across the street on their own. There is no fear in climbing a structure that is too high for them and on which they cannot hold on, because they've yet to experience the pain of falling and hitting the ground. In adolescence, this pride results from a false belief about what they know—and what their parents don't! It is, indeed, human nature to not want to depend on anyone else. Dependency feels weak and vulnerable. To depend on you, I must trust you. What if you are not trustworthy? I'm safer depending on myself, we believe. All the more so in terms of trusting a God who is Spirit and whom we cannot see.

Sooner or later, reality comes crashing through for all of us. **We experience that we don't know as much as we thought we knew, and we certainly cannot control the circumstances of life as we want. This is the root of all anxiety.**

When we are first introduced to Eve in the garden, she is in a state of blissful childlike dependence on God. It is when Satan suggests to her that she can be independent of God and make her own choices that her will kicks in. Her pride is awakened. Her choice to not trust God and go outside the bounds of her created design resulted in a severed relationship. Reality came crashing down upon her quickly, and she realized she didn't have the ability to be God. Fear and anxiety were immediate results, and we see her running away from God to hide, instead of running to Him for comfort. **Her pride was certainly a problem, but it was what the pride led to that was the bigger problem: a lack of ability to trust.**

Rebellion vs. trust

Our rebellion *to* Him comes out of a lack of trust *in* Him. When we rebel, we are saying with our lives, "I don't want you to tell me what to do! I will make my own choices. You don't know or care what is truly best for me!" We are agreeing with Satan that the Lord is a liar and that He is not good. If we truly believe that He is good, knows all things including what's best for us, loves us with unconditional love, and is the most powerful being in the universe, we would rest in His care and gladly follow His directions just like my grandson.

Rebellion is our judgment on His holiness. Trusting (or not) is our choice, our responsibility. The Lord asks Adam and Eve, the disciples, and us, "Who do you say that I am" (Matthew 16:15)? Who we choose to trust shapes our behavior and directs the course of our lives. In the end, I believe it's that choice—**who** we trusted—not simply what we did, that we will be judged for when we stand before Him.

Connection and trust

When trust is severed, relationship is severed. *You cannot be in relationship with someone you do not trust.* In her mistrust of God, Eve severed their relationship. Being severed from the source of life led to immediate spiritual death and eventual physical death.

You might think, "Wait a minute, Satan was actually right about one thing. Eve didn't die." A deeper reflection will cause us to consider the broader question. What truly is life and death? Jesus tells us, "Life is more than food" (Luke 12:23). He expounds on this throughout all of Scripture and very clearly with the woman at the well: "If you knew the gift of God and who it is who says to you, 'Give me a drink,' you would have asked Him, and He would have given you living water. Everyone who drinks this water shall thirst again; but whoever drinks the water I will give him shall have it springing up within him as a well of living water to eternal life" (John 4:10-14).

Taken as a whole, Scripture tells us that the life God gives us is eternal. It comes from living in an intimate, loving relationship with Him where the mystery of the physical realm (us in bodily form) and the spiritual realm (Him in Spirit) are united. The result of living in this relationship is all the fruits of the Spirit (love, joy, peace, patience, kindness, goodness, faithfulness, gentleness, self-control). It's abundant. It's filled with His blessings and good gifts. And it overflows with love to all other human beings and all of creation. This is how Jesus defines life.

I don't know how much Eve knew or understood about eternal life at this point in the garden. But she did know that God had provided everything for her to live up to that point. When Satan enters the picture and challenges God's character, he redefines "life." He tells her, "Life is you deciding for yourself what is wise and good and best for you." That sure sounds good. But the results were devastating. Broken relationship with her creator and the source of life, dissension with her husband, shame, fear, blaming, and feeling vulnerable. These were real and immediate emotional, relational, behavioral, and spiritual consequences. Based on current neuroscience research, we can also assume there were physiological implications as well. We are integrated beings, and our thoughts have neurochemical, hormonal, and muscular responses. Adam also experienced all these consequences as soon as he made the same fatal decision. And clearly, these consequences continued on with their children and children's children down to us.

Implicitly, Satan defined death as physical death. God defined it as not living in intimacy and peace with Him and others. Conversely, Satan implies life is you getting to be your own god and deciding for yourself what is good and evil. God says life is trusting Me and My Word, living in obedience to it, and thus, in harmony with Me and others. It's much more than physical life. Life necessitates being connected to the source of life. Much like someone being hooked up to life support, once that's unplugged, though a body is still present, they are declared dead.

The rest of human history and the rest of the Bible tell the story of God pursuing relationship with His broken and estranged children. He goes to every length to "show and tell" that He is God and He is good. That He is actually **for them not against them**. That He loves them and longs to bring them back into relationship with Him. He wants us to trust His character, His love, His goodness, and His interpretation of reality and our circumstances. "I am the Good Shepherd, and I come to lay down my life for the sheep" (John 10:11). He performs all His great works to show His character and earn our trust!

If we accept Satan's definition of God (not good), we will understand His response to Adam and Eve as **vindictive**. If we accept God's own description of His character (good), we will see His response to them as **natural consequences and tough love**. When we have adult children who choose not to trust our advice and do not want to be in relationship with us, our heart breaks. Yet we give them the freedom to choose and watch with heavy hearts as they experience the very things we were trying to spare them from.

This might be a stretch, but I think Eve's resulting pain in childbirth is also a natural consequence. "Give attention to My words and obey them, for they are life to those who find them and health to their whole body" (Proverbs 4:20-23). There is much research out there that clearly shows a direct correlation between our thought life (mental health) and our physical health. Gut issues, inflammation, rheumatoid arthritis, heart issues, etc. can all be related to our states of stress and anxiety. I believe Eve's decision to not trust the creator and source of life had physical implications as well.

Adam's struggle with farming and the earth is also a natural consequence. One of humanity's main jobs was to be caretakers of the earth and the animals. Adam and Eve's choice not to trust God and live in relationship with Him impacted all of creation. "Creation itself will also be set free from its slavery to corruption into the freedom of the glory of the children of God. For we know that the whole creation groans and suffers the pains of childbirth until now" (Romans 8:19-22).

Again, humanity is designed to be in community: first with the Triune God, then with all of humanity, and also with all of creation. Our choices have real impacts on all levels of this community. In our minds, we tend to understand ourselves as isolated entities. "What I choose is my own business, it has no impact on you" says our "live and let live" philosophy of the day. Nothing could be further from the truth.

And God's decision to remove Adam and Eve from the garden is pure love and mercy. In their current state of estrangement from God and making the choice to not trust Him, Adam and Eve are left in an extremely dangerous position. Why would they choose to trust God with what He said about the tree of eternal life? If they decided to make up their own minds about that tree and eat from it, that would mean choosing eternal life in brokenness without any hope of healing and redemption. God could not let that happen.

Eve's lack of trust led to lack of connection with the creator of her soul. She suffered the consequences of a broken relationship. Alone, full of shame and scared, she ran to further isolate and hide. She could not go to God to be comforted in her time of need. Nor could she receive His wisdom about all she did not know, because she had cut herself off from that relationship.

Whose definition of God do we trust? This is a crucial question and takes some intentional and prayerful meditation to answer truthfully. The answer has profound implications for our life. "The lamp of the body is the eye; if therefore your eye is clear, your whole body will be full of light. But if your eye is bad, your whole body will be full of darkness" (Matthew 6:22-23).

The "eye" here is what we see, how we understand reality and our circumstances. **How we see and understand God will determine how we relate to Him,** whether we choose to pursue Him as a child does her wonderful Father, as one would a lover, or whether we do enough to appease Him but try to stay out of His purview lest we incur His wrath. It will determine whether we trust Him or not.

God has told us that He alone is God, He is the creator of heaven and earth, He is the only Savior, He is good, He is kind, He is holy, He is just, He is patient, He is full of compassion, mercy, and grace. He cannot lie. Heaven and earth will pass away, but every single Word He has spoken will be fulfilled.

Furthermore, He tells us that the enemy—His enemy and our enemy—roars about like a lion seeking someone to devour (1 Peter 5:8). His job description is to steal, kill, and destroy (John 10:10). His character "was a murderer from the beginning, and he does not stand in the truth, because there is no truth in him. Whenever he speaks a lie, he speaks from his own nature, for he is a liar and the father of lies" (John 8:44).

Satan tells us God is not good. God is the liar. He is a jealous, egotistical, vindictive narcissist.

They both can't be right. Only one is telling the truth. Whom do you trust? This is the question of the story of Adam and Eve. The same question rings through the ages down to us.

CHAPTER 2 MEDITATIONS

1. Think about how you interpret the story of Adam and Eve. What are the assumptions—likely subconscious—you've made about God here? What aspects of His character have been highlighted to you? What do think the story is really about? How do you understand God's responses to them?

2. Try substituting the word "trust" whenever you see the words "faith"' or "belief" in Scripture. Does it make a difference in how you understand the passage? How?

3. Can you identify any areas of your life where the enemy is whispering to you, "Did God really say…? That's not true. That won't happen!"

4. How do you define "life" and "death"? Does your life reflect this understanding?

5. Have you ever considered the idea that when you don't trust God, you're calling Him a liar?

6. Think about those in your life with whom you're supposed to be in relationship. Consider the role of trust in those relationships and how it impacts your intimacy and your desire to pursue them.

7. What are the current circumstances in your life that are difficult for you? How do you "see" and "understand" them? Who are you allowing to

define your "objective reality"? Where is God in these circumstances?

8. Can you identify any patterns in areas of your life that are difficult to trust the Lord with?

9. What passages of Scripture are difficult for you to trust God with?

10. Do you think there might be a correlation between your physical health and your relationship with God?

Chapter 2 References

1. Reconditioning the Nervous System from Fear and Abandonment, webinar by Stephen Porges through NICABM (National Institute for the Clinical Application of Behavioral Medicine) (2024)
2. *Affect Regulation and the Origin of the Self,* first edition, by Allan N. Schore, Ph.D. (2015)
3. *The Developing Mind,* by Daniel J. Siegel, M.D. (1999)
4. How Childhood Trauma Affects Health Across a Lifetime, Ted Talk by Nadine Burke Harris; https://youtu.be/95ovIJ3dsNk (2015)

How Broken Trust Became Generational Dysfunction

Insecure attachment styles and how they impact relationships with God and others

We left Adam and Eve in the garden in a miserable state. Their decision to cease trusting their Father caused a broken relationship with the source of life. They pulled the plug from their own life support system. Now they are on their own. This is what they thought they wanted, but very quickly they realize they are ill equipped to navigate this life.

Eve: "I'm naked. What do I do? How do I make clothes? What was I thinking? I've been duped. How could I have been so stupid?"

Adam: "I can't create seeds or food! How do I know how much rain or sun is needed? How do I deal with all these animals and bugs?"

Eve: "I feel so scared and overwhelmed. How did we get here? It's your fault! You didn't warn me about that blasted snake!"

Adam: "You didn't listen to me. I told you exactly what the Father told me! It's YOUR fault."

We can imagine the dialogue and the panic. The honeymoon phase is definitely over. Adam's awe and joy of being given the gift of "bone of my bone and flesh of my flesh" has turned into Eve becoming a burden that has messed up his life. And Adam is no longer the knight in shining armor for Eve. His blaming and lack of protection are infuriating. Whatever else is going on between them, we clearly see that their original harmony is replaced with blaming, anger, fear, and shame. Both respond with self-protective, defensive behaviors toward each other. They can no longer trust each other.

We all know the saying that "hurt people hurt people." It's true. When we are wounded and uncared for in the ways we most need to be, our instinctual response is to become more self-focused and self-absorbed. If we are truly on our own, how else will we survive? All of our internal and external reserves are harnessed to take care of ourselves, even at the expense of others. **We simply cannot and will not give of ourselves to others unless we are sure at a core level we are safe (physically and emotionally) and able to survive. Jesus' ability to be completely** present—in every moment—was directly correlated with His total lack of worry or distraction over His safety or provision—in every moment. His all-encompassing trust in the Father was unwavering.

I don't want to get bogged down here in the minutiae of Adam and Eve's parenting. But I do want to highlight that I believe in their newly wounded state, they were unable to be present for their children in the way the Father originally desired. I don't want to blame them for Cain's ultimate free-will, horrible life choices. After all, even the perfect Father has many prodigal sons and daughters. Nevertheless, I think we can all admit that none of us had perfect parents, none of us are perfect parents, and that this impacts us and our children in ways both small and profound.

Let us now return to the Attachment Cycle and see how our wounds can impact future generations.

Remember that the Attachment Cycle is the dance we have with our primary caregivers that teaches us about who we are, what the world is like, and how to do relationships. We learn all this through how they care for us and meet our needs. The messages we learn in this dance actually get wired neurologically into our brains, impacting our brain development and physiological states, and our muscles, joints, immune systems, organs, etc. They give us a pair of lenses through which we now see the world, interpret current circumstances, and anticipate the future.

The brokenness of our primary caregivers impacts the way they enter into the attachment dance with us and meet our needs. In turn, this impacts what gets wired into our brains about our identities, the world, and how to do relationships, and whether or not we can trust them. It influences how we parent our children and creates generational dysfunctions unless we heal. What we understand about all of this in the physical realm impacts how we understand and relate to the Father in the spiritual realm.

In Chapter 1, we looked at how the Attachment Cycle is designed to work resulting in a Secure Attachment style for children. When our primary caregivers are wounded and unable to care for us in adequate, predictable, or nurturing ways, the result will be the development of an insecure attachment style.

There are three types of insecure attachment: Avoidant Attachment, Ambivalent Attachment, and Disorganized Attachment.

Avoidant Attachment
If a caregiver is emotionally unavailable and does not engage the infant on an emotional level, the infant will not receive the messages of being seen, heard, or comforted. Physical needs may be sufficiently met, but emotional

needs are minimized or ignored. Perhaps the caregiver has been led to believe that infants can't really process emotions. This was the prevailing thought which impacted parenting in Western culture up until the 1970s. Despite a plethora of research to the contrary, it remains a prevailing view in much of the Western church. Other times, caregivers minimize the emotional needs of their infants because they don't really know how to deal with them. Emotions are very uncomfortable for them.

My mother was the fourth of five children who grew up during the Depression in a family of German heritage. Life was tough. Her parents did not have much time or energy for comforting their children as they were trying to put food on the table and provide shelter and clothes. She learned to simply ignore her emotional pain and "get on with it." So that is how she parented me. When I tried to engage her on an emotional level as a teenager, she responded, "Melinda, I'm German and we don't do emotions."

In this situation, the infant learns to ignore her own emotions. She learns to distract herself when emotional needs arise. In infancy, that means focusing her attention on her toys. As an adult, she could distract herself with food, work, exercise, shopping … anything. But she has become "programmed" to not go to others with emotional needs nor engage on an emotional level. She has learned to push those needs out of consciousness and distract herself from paying attention to them.

These children are often the ones identified as very independent. They don't cry when separated from a caregiver and can look cool as a cucumber. They tend to be easier to take care of since they are not fussy, whiny, or needy. These children have already learned at a very young age that they are on their own to try to manage their emotional needs. But research blows their cover. When cortisol levels (stress hormones) are measured in these kids, they are shown to be consistently higher than the levels in other more obviously distraught children. They simply learn to mask their stress.

Since this child's emotional needs have not been seen or attended to by a caregiver, she experiences her inner life as invisible and unimportant to others. Though these babies can grow up to be quite functional adults, this emotional piece is compromised in relationships. Because she learned to cut herself off from her own emotional life, it is very difficult for her to enter into the emotional lives of others. In this way, she repeats the pattern of emotional unavailability to the next generation. As with my mother, caregivers who were emotionally unavailable almost certainly were raised by those with the same limitations.

Summary of Avoidant Attachment

- **Messages:** Only behaviors matter. Who you are on the inside is not important or seen.
- **Lenses of perception:** What you think, feel, and want do not matter to others and will not be attended to.
- **Anticipation of future:** You have to deal with your inner thoughts and feelings on your own. Others will not meet your emotional needs.
- **Body and brain:** Body has no muscle memory of being comforted and emotionally regulated. Being left in emotional distress to deal with it on your own results in anxiety and accompanying muscle tension, an elevated heart rate, and being quick to react and fly off the handle.
- Brain is developed around fight, flight, freeze survival skills versus learning and connection.
- **Social:** You relate to others on a superficial level and through activities, not on an emotional level. You have an undeveloped emotional vocabulary and difficulty seeing others emotionally.

Note: Emotions are the **color** and **connectors** of life. They give a depth and richness to life experiences, both positive and negative. They connect us to ourselves and others. **Without an emotional component, we cannot function as fully human.**

You can see how this would translate to obstacles in trusting the Father. It becomes very difficult to believe He really cares about how you feel. You assume, consciously or subconsciously, that He is only really concerned about your behaviors. You might obey Him, but your heart is far from Him.

Ambivalent Attachment

Sometimes caregivers will meet the needs of an infant in an unpredictable way. At times they are present (physically or emotionally), and at times they are not.

Think about caregivers who may have mental illnesses, or use substances, or are single caregivers with no help. This is in no way to judge such caregivers. It is simply to give examples of how an Ambivalent Attachment style develops. In such situations, the baby has no idea when the caregiver is available for him or not.

The pattern developed here is one of "the squeaky wheel gets the grease." He figures out that he needs to cry long and hard to get and keep the attention of his caregiver. If he ceases crying, chances are he will not be paid attention to. This translates in adulthood into needing to be in control in relationships. The tendency is to become an expert at reading the room, doing things to stay in the center of attention, or learning how to manipulate relationships so that your needs are met. Relationships have an anxious, needy tone because the person is not confident about whether the other person will consistently be there.

As these children grow up, they tend to become parents who continue to be controlling. You can see this in the ways they play with their younger children. It's difficult for these parents to let the kids simply "free play" and make up their own rules.

When you scratch below the surface, it becomes clear that interactions with their children are often performed to meet their own needs instead of those of the kids. A father might attempt to hold an infant or young child beyond what the child wants in an effort to keep the child close and get his own needs for comfort met. Again, these parents have learned that the only consistent way they are going to get their own needs met is if they are manipulative and controlling.

Children parented by those with an Ambivalent Attachment respond ambivalently. They have this "push-pull" relationship, wanting to be close but pulling away when they feel controlled or smothered. Such an ambivalent response to the parent triggers the parent's wounds of unpredictability about getting their own needs met, and they may try to cling to the child or control them harder.

The child's ambivalent response is carried into how they develop relationships and do their own parenting in the future.

Summary of Ambivalent Attachment:
- **Messages:** You cannot count on people to be there for you. They might be; they might not be. You have to stay in the focus of attention if you want to get your needs met. You need to control the situation.
- **Lenses of perception:** The world and relationships are very unpredictable.
- **Anticipation of future:** Unpredictability. If you have something now, hold on. It may not last.
- **Body and brain:** Body is in a state of constant distress and resulting anxiety.
- Brain is developed around fight, flight, freeze survival skills versus learning and connection.
- **Social:** You learn how to manipulate relationships to get your own needs met. You have underlying anger toward others because you aren't confident you can count on them. Fears of rejection are easily triggered.

In your relationship with God, this can look like being anxious about whether or not He will meet your need **this** time. You may even be able to recount many ways He has answered prayer in the past, but that doesn't mean He will answer this time! There may be a sense of needing to bargain with Him: "Lord, I promise to read my Bible more often if you please, please, please answer this prayer!" Or "Lord, I will stop watching pornography if you just help me get this job!"

Other times it might result in a sense of striving: a sense of needing to do more and check more boxes in an effort to manipulate God into paying attention to you and your needs or requests. Your spiritual life resembles the life of the doubter that James describes (James 1:5-6). Your internal state is like the waves of the sea driven and tossed about by the wind. Absent from your relationship with God are a sense of peace, rest, stillness, and confidence in His predictable love.

Disorganized Attachment

The last insecure attachment style is Disorganized Attachment. This is developed when a caregiver is threatening to an infant as in situations of physical, sexual, or emotional abuse.

God designed all mammals to "go to" their primary caregivers for comfort and protection when they have needs or are under stress. Mammals are also designed to "run away" from threats. If the infant is scared or has any needs, but the caregiver is threatening, the infant does not know what to do. Do I go to the caregiver or run away? This causes a splitting within the infant. It results in a disconnect between different parts of the brain or between the brain and body. The infant has no coherent strategy about how to relate to others or get their needs met and has no coherent sense of self.

If the caregiver is mostly absent or neglectful, this is also experienced by the infant as threatening. We have a primal need to be safe and cannot survive without others. Thus, our core instinctual fear is being left alone. Left in isolation, we have no one to help us or to whom we can bring our needs.

A child raised in such an environment has a nervous system that never gets the opportunity to be co-regulated and re-set to "calm." She is left to deal with these scary and threatening emotions on her own without any knowledge or ability to do so. The result is overwhelming fear and anxiety. Any future real or perceived hints of abandonment will trigger multiple fear responses physiologically, cognitively, and behaviorally. Loneliness and isolation are root causes in anxiety. Alone, we cannot communicate our needs or get help to regulate ourselves.

As the child gets older, this can look like dissociative disorders or other personality disorders. Relationships are very chaotic, and the ability to live a stable life is compromised. We see ourselves by looking in a mirror. Our first mirror is the eyes of our caregiver. If no eyes are looking back at us, it is impossible to know who we are. If angry eyes are looking at us, we encode a sense of shame.

When children are raised by those with a Disorganized Attachment, they develop this same attachment themselves. In raising their own children, they repeat the cycle of abuse or neglect not knowing what else to do.

Summary of Disorganized Attachment:
- **Messages:** Something is wrong with you. You are not liked. You are not worth being cared for.
- **Lenses of perception:** Relationships are incoherent. The world is terrifying.
- **Anticipation of future:** Chaos and confusion.
- **Body and brain:** Body is in a state of constant distress.
- Brain is developed around fight, flight, freeze survival skills versus learning and connection.
- **Social:** You have no idea how to navigate relationships, be intimate, or ask for your own needs. You often experience a revolving door of chaotic and dysfunctional relationships. You may slip into detachment from your own brain and reality, like a schizophrenic or catatonic mental illness, or into

isolation from the rest of humanity, like becoming unhoused.

If you have a Disorganized Attachment style, relating to Father God is terrifying. You will expect Him to be neglectful, not paying any attention to you unless He decides He wants to unleash wrath upon you. Certainly, this is not a God you would willingly draw near to or trust.

Any attempts by others to talk to you about God would likely be rebuffed. You would probably just shut down or walk away. It would not be surprising if simply going into a church building would cause anxiety or a sense of being threatened.

For those who struggle with a Disorganized Attachment style, trust is very hard to learn. It usually requires the help of a counselor or gifted mentor who understands the nuances of attachment styles and effective interventions.

More about the importance of "Voice"
As I have hinted at previously, the concept of "voice" is very important in the development of trust and the formation of our identity. It's a central part of being created in the image of God, who is also called The Word of God. God speaks; therefore, we speak.

All of the insecure attachment styles impede the infant's voice in one way or another. When a baby's cries are ignored or become ineffective in getting their needs met, they are left with only one alternative, to use their behavior in some way. (Note: I'm not talking about attending to cries 100% of the time. That's impossible. Rather, I'm talking about an overall pattern of care.) As I've often heard, "Behavior is the language of those who have lost their voice." Quite often, children's misbehaviors are developed subconsciously. It's instinctual to our survival to attempt to meet our needs. It bears repeating, if we can't use our voice to get our needs met, we will find other ways.

Stealing one's voice is of the enemy. If we don't know how to use our voice, we cannot be in relationship with God or others. Learning to use our voice in adult and constructive ways is a huge part of reclaiming our God-given dignity, power, and identity. Learning to give others their voice back who have lost it is a powerful way to practically love and value them.

More about the importance of Co-Regulation

The concept of "Co-Regulation" simply means I need help to be "regulated" or calmed. A baby has no ability to calm themselves when they are upset. Someone must calm them. It involves holding them, talking to them with soothing words and in a soothing voice, assuring them you are there and that they will be OK. It involves meeting whatever need they have; changing a diaper, feeding them, or shooing away the scary dog, for example. When a baby is calmed, their nervous system is reset. Muscles go from a position of tension to relaxation. Stress hormones are replaced by calming hormones. All of this is going on at a physiological and chemical level.

Caregivers who parent with any of the three insecure attachment styles hamper this process of co-regulation. When infants are not co-regulated, or calmed, they are left in a state of stress. Their muscles remain in a state of tension and stress hormones continue to be pumped through their brains into their bodies. This has serious consequences for ongoing brain development and physical health. The longer one is left in a state of dysregulation and is not being comforted by others, the more serious the consequences will be neurologically, physiologically, and socially. People cannot function in such states of stress. In the absence of others comfort, we will find whatever we can to take away our pain and anxiety; drugs, alcohol, sex, food etc. It's not surprising that one of the primary expressions of God's nature is His desire and ability to comfort us, His children (2 Corinthians 1:3-4). He wants us to experience this comfort from Him. Our human relationships can make this easier or harder to receive.

Chapter summary: The essence of trust

The essence of our ability to trust is based on how we were cared for and valued. **My ability to trust you is inextricably connected to you valuing me, hearing my voice, and meeting my needs.** Trust within relationships is not a given. It is conditional. It must be earned.

Think about this. I won't trust you if you don't take care of me. I won't trust you if you do not value me. I won't trust you if you are not for me. This implies your **intentions** toward me are **good,** and that you have the **ability, power, and will** to follow through on those intentions and actually take care of me. Good intentions without actions are not enough. As the saying goes, that's what the road to hell is paved with.

Furthermore, if I trust you, **my identity is secure with you**. I know I am loved and valued by you. I know you will do your best to comfort me and meet my needs.

Where there is trust, I am free to be fully me. In the absence of trust, a dysfunctional dance is present. My voice is silenced in some way. I need to hide my thoughts and emotions to protect myself from negative or even threatening responses from others. This need to hide or suppress my emotions can lead me to dissociate or find other forms of distraction. It all takes enormous amounts of energy and leaves me feeling anxious.

Take a minute to ponder how this all works out for you in your human relationships. Then consider how you experience each of these components in your relationship with the Father.

For some, this review of attachment styles and how trust is developed may open a can of worms. Hard feelings toward caregivers might arise. But remember, your primary caregiver also has his or her own story. This section is not about laying blame. It's about developing understanding and gaining a new perspective. In my own life, this has led to increased compassion and a greater ability to offer grace and forgiveness to others. My prayer is that the same will be true for you.

My point here is to communicate that there are well-defined aspects of our early development that impact our ability to trust others. These aspects are mostly subconscious but can become conscious with some intentional reflection.

These patterns also profoundly impact our relationship with God and often become the stumbling blocks for experiencing deep intimacy with Him. We tend to think that our relationship with God is, or can be, totally separate from our relationships with humanity. **The reality is that our relationships with humanity become the prism through which we are predisposed to understand and**

relate to God. We will attach to God in the same way we attach to humans.

Jesus clearly tells us, "If someone says, 'I love God,' and hates his brother, he is a liar; for the one who does not love his brother whom he has seen, cannot love God whom he has not seen" (I John 4:20). This is an intentional design by our kind Creator. His heart was to give us a physical experience of a spiritual reality, a visible sign of the invisible truth. This is why **all** His commands are summed up in one sentence "You shall love your neighbor as yourself" (Galatians 5:14).

God wants us to love each other the way He loves us. The way we treat others is meant to be a perfect reflection of how He treats us. The very first place this was to happen was between parents and children through the Attachment Cycle. God's design was for parents to perfectly meet the needs of their children—adequately, predictably, and emotionally. In this way, an infant would develop a secure attachment and learn his worth and identity. He would be predisposed to attach to, trust, and value others. This would be the legacy passed on to future generations in his own parenting. A ripple effect of love, life, care, and comfort would be sown within communities. And a child would experience a perfect physical example of his Heavenly Father, thus setting him up to easily trust Him.

When caregivers don't do this but wound us instead, we carry our wounds forward in the way we insecurely parent the next generation. And so, the cycle of dysfunction has been translated down through the ages. And we become predisposed **not** to trust the Lord either.

CHAPTER 3 MEDITATIONS

1. Think about your own upbringing. Was your primary caregiver emotionally present and attuned to you? Did they "see" your inner life and give validity to that?

2. Were you allowed to have emotions in your family? Only positive ones? Only anger?

3. How were emotions dealt with in your family?

4. How did your primary caregiver respond to your feelings of emotional pain? Anger? Loneliness? Fear? Joy? Happiness? Excitement?

5. Are you aware of your emotions, or do you tend to minimize and ignore them? Do you attempt to hide them to avoid a negative response from others? If so, how do you tend to distract yourself?

6. Who or what do you go to when you need comfort?

7. On a scale of 1-5, 5 being most comfortable, how comfortable are you in engaging with others on an emotional level?

8. Did your primary caregiver meet your needs in a predictable way?

9. Did your primary caregiver meet your needs in adequate ways?

10. Do you struggle with fears of abandonment?

11. Do you struggle with being manipulative or controlling in relationships in an attempt to get your needs met?
12. Do you struggle with feeling needy in relationships?
13. Was your primary caregiver neglectful or threatening to you?
14. Would you describe your relationship with the Lord as Secure (you can rest in His care), Avoidant (you struggle with believing He sees you or cares about your heart), Ambivalent (you're anxious about His predictability), or Disorganized (you fear His wrath)? Maybe you vacillate between them all. Note: Read on for steps of healing.

Chapter 3 References

1. Trust-Based Relational Intervention® from the original Participants Workbooks: *TBRI® Introduction and Overview, TBRI® Connecting Principles, TBRI® Empowering Principles,* and *TBRI® Correcting Principles,* by Purvis, K.; Cross, D.R.; Hurst, J.R.; Milton, H. (2013)
2. Reconditioning the Nervous System from Fear and Abandonment, webinar by Stephen Porges through NICABM (National Institute for the Clinical Application of Behavioral Medicine) (2024)
3. *The Power of Showing Up,* by Daniel J. Siegel, M.D., and Tina Payne Bryson, Ph.D. (2021)
4. *Affect Regulation and the Origin of the Self,* first edition, by Allan N. Schore, Ph.D. (2015)
5. *The Developing Mind,* by Daniel J. Siegel, M.D. (1999)
6. The Strange Situation experiment, by Mary Ainsworth, Ph.D., YouTube
7. The Still Face experiment, by Edward Tronick, Ph.D., YouTube
8. Rhesus monkey studies, by Harry Harlow, Ph.D., YouTube

CORRECTIVE EXPERIENCES FROM GOD TO REGAIN TRUST

LEARNING THE CHARACTER OF GOD THROUGH EXPERIENCES

We were created to be in perfect communion with the Triune God and each other. But this perfect communion was severed when humanity ceased to trust Him, His character, and goodness and chose rather to believe the lies presented by someone they did not know (the snake in the Garden). Now they would live estranged from God. In addition, being cut off from their source of life had catastrophic consequences within Adam and Eve individually, between them, and that they passed on to future generations.

Broken relationships needed to be addressed on two levels: a spiritual level between God and man and a physical level between the creatures themselves. Healing must occur on both levels for us to live the lives we were meant to live. It doesn't really matter where you start, as healing on one level will impact healing on the other. It only matters that at some point you address both your spiritual and your physical relationships. For some of us, it's easier to start this healing process with our relationship with God. For others, it's easier to start by addressing our need for healing with other humans. In the next two sections, we will look at the healing process on both levels: with God and with humanity.

Let's start by looking at our need for healing with our Creator. How do we go about learning to know and trust Him?

I believe the most devastating result of The Fall of humanity was the separation of the physical and spiritual realm in a significant yet mysterious way. Before The Fall, God, who is Spirit, is walking around in the physical garden. Adam and Eve are able to interact with Him in meaningful ways. There seems to be no disconnect between the spirit world and their physical world. It's only after The Fall, when they are lovingly kicked out of the garden, that we see this disconnect.

The garden and the tree of life represent the eternal, spiritual, yet very tangible Kingdom of God. Adam and Eve have lost direct access to this. Now they are stuck in this very frustrating reality of the physical realm being separated from the spiritual realm. God is experienced as distant.

The reality of a spiritual world beyond what we can see, taste, or touch is both known and hoped for by us all. It is sewn within the human DNA. Anyone who has ever stood by the casket of a loved one and peered into their lifeless body groans with the deepest groans known to man, "This can't be all there is." It always fascinates me how those who "poo-poo" a spiritual realm as akin to tribal superstitions will so readily embrace the reality of the paranormal or go to a tarot card reader who brings up the dead. We know there's more to life and reality than we can see.

So what is God to do with His children in their current state? How can He heal them? Prove His character? Teach them how to live in this disconnected reality? The rest of history is His answer. Over and over, throughout the ages, He gives humanity a chance at a re-do. It's as if He's saying, "Let's try this again. Trust me!"

He places individuals, kings, and nations in the position of a dependent infant to learn the lessons of a secure attachment style. He gives them "corrective experiences", new experiences to correct their wrong thinking. **He doesn't just tell them; He shows them. He says, "Taste and see that the Lord is good"** (Psalm 34:8).

In their physical realm, He shows humanity spiritual realities: about Him, His character, life, and death. The culmination is the incarnation, death, and resurrection of

Jesus. Through Him, the Father reconnects the physical and spiritual world in a profound but not yet complete way. Jesus is fully God and fully man (Colossians 2:9). He is the image of the invisible God (Colossians 1:15) and shows us a perfect representation of who the Father is. Any questions we have about the Father's goodness or character are answered definitively in the life and words of Jesus.

All of history and the entire Bible are a study of these corrective experiences. Let's look at the example of Abraham.

Abraham and Israel: Trusting God's provision, power, and intentions

God decides to show His character and goodness to the world by choosing one man, Abraham, and developing a deeply intimate relationship with him. Not only would God bless Abraham, He would use him to bless the whole world. He would also use their relationship to show the world that what Satan had said about Him was a lie.

It's important to note that God is the one who initiates this relationship. Kids cannot initiate relationship with parents. Parents must be the ones to initiate and teach kids about their identity, life, and how to relate in the world through the attachment dance.

God comes to Abraham and tells him to leave his home, his relatives, everything he's known, and come with Him on an adventure. God promised He would give him land—the best land possible—and enough children to work the land and become a great nation. He would use him to bless all the world and protect him from those who wanted to hurt him. God would give Abraham everything he needed, in fact, more than he could even imagine.

Abraham had to consider many things. Did God actually know where such great land was and how to get there? Was He able to give him all these children? After all, at 75 he still had none. Could He really protect him from man and beast and every other potential peril? How could He possibly use him to bless the whole world? Think about the character traits God is displaying about Himself in this dialogue. Wisdom, power, and goodness! He comes to Abraham with a heart full of good intentions for him, his family, and the whole world!

He will provide for him, protect him, and be with him along the way. All the messages of Felt-Safety necessary for developing a Secure Attachment style are present.

God is communicating to Abraham: "I know the plans that I have for you. Plans for welfare and not calamity, to give you a future and a hope" (Jeremiah 29:11). These traits are in direct opposition to how Satan portrayed God to Eve in the garden. We know the story, so it's easy to overlook the drama here. But **Abraham has a real choice. It's not an easy choice.**

Look again at Romans 4:16-22. Abraham is mulling these things over. After considering everything, he comes to the conclusion, "being fully assured that what God promised, He was able to do" (v. 21). Abraham chooses to trust God, to trust that what He revealed about Himself was true, and that somehow, He was able to make good on all those promises. **As a result of this trust, Abraham obeyed and set out to parts unknown, putting himself in an utterly infant-like dependency on the Lord.** It was his TRUST in God that pleased the Father so much and allowed Him to unleash all His blessings upon him.

Life—abundant life, eternal life—is only experienced through obedience and submission to God and His Word. And this is where many of us get tripped up. For most of us, the word obedience conjures up thoughts and images of fear and punishment. Submission is even worse, causing us to imagine pictures of oppression and slavery. **In our minds, obedience and submission are disconnected from notions of trust, love, and goodness. God's desire is that they are intimately connected.** We may choose to obey God out of fear, but that type of obedience does not lead to intimacy.

The Lord wants intimacy with us. He desires an obedience that is borne out of this relationship and trust. And that means trusting His goodness. "Without faith (trust), it is impossible to please Him, for he who comes to God must believe that He is and **that He is a rewarder of those who seek Him"** (Hebrews 11:6). The Psalms and prophets are replete with warnings and blessings depending on whether or not one trusts the Lord—or mankind or idols or other false teachers.

The story of Abraham takes a long time to unfold, centuries in fact. But the Lord told this to Abraham in advance (Genesis 15). This is a beautiful example of the Lord being predictable. He always reveals His plans to His servants before He does them (Amos 3:7). In the interim, the Lord is not sleeping. He's working to prepare His people for all that He has for them. He has many other lessons for them to learn to cement their knowledge of who He is so that when the time comes, they will be able to continue to trust Him.

Abraham's initial choice to trust the Lord with all He promised has proven to be a good move. The Lord has indeed shown him the way to this promised land of milk and honey (Genesis 13). God has prospered and protected him at every turn. **Abraham has learned by experience that the Lord means what He says and is able to fulfill all His promises to him.** It is this foundation of relational experience with God that allows Abraham to continue to trust God in one of the most extraordinary situations of his life.

Some years after having finally received the son of promise at age 100, Abraham is told by God to sacrifice him (Genesis 22). We know that God didn't truly intend for Abraham to do this, it was just a test to see if Abraham would trust Him. But Abraham didn't know this. Can you imagine? To get the full weight of what is being taught here, we must put ourselves in the story. We miss so much by simply glossing over the words.

Scripture tells us two reasons Abraham was able to trust God even in this. Genesis 22:14 says that Abraham trusted God to provide. It didn't make sense, but somehow this God who gave him and Sarah a son long after child-bearing ages could do anything. Isaac was just the beginning of the fulfillment of His promise. God had to come through some way. Hebrews 11:19 and Romans 4:17 tell us Abraham also thought that even if God killed Isaac, He was able to raise him from the dead. Incredible! How did Abraham even think this thought? There's no evidence that anyone up to this point in history had ever risen from the dead!

Again, Abraham had learned the heart and character of the Father through relational experience with Him. He saw and began to understand that God was good. He was able to provide and protect. He was much wiser than Abraham and able to do things impossible for Abraham to do. Whatever He says, will be. He could be trusted.

This unwavering trust in his Father God allowed Abraham to walk in intimacy and security with Him all his days. It allowed the blessings of God to continue to flow to him and his descendants. The legacy of trust, the experiential knowledge of God was passed to each successive generation. His mighty deeds were told, sung about, written down, and celebrated in festivals. When a new generation believed the testimonies of their fathers, then they too trusted the Lord. And their trust allowed them to live in intimacy and security with the Lord and receive their own experiences of blessing. It allowed them to affirm for themselves the goodness, kindness, wisdom, and power of God.

Common obstacles to trusting the Lord

The rest of Scripture tells the story of humanity through the ages, contrasting the lives of those who choose to trust the Lord and those who don't. **Trusting the Lord always results in experiencing an intimate, secure relationship with Him. It inevitably leads to many blessings, though usually not immediately and not without suffering and struggle.** What leads some to trust and others not to? Let's consider some of the common obstacles often experienced that hinder trusting the Lord.

1. Circumstances: The story of Joseph

If you remember Satan's scheme to deceive Eve in the garden, you will recall that he redefines her "objective circumstances," the apple. It's just an apple. But God says it's dangerous and not to be eaten. Satan says it's good and desirable to make her wise. **It bears repeating that what we see is determined by what we hear.** Perspective is everything.

Some of us are "glass half-full people" and some "glass half-empty" people. What's the difference? Much more than the actual details of our lives, it's how we interpret or make sense of them that impacts us. This is where our attachment styles come in to play. If your past experiences create a running voice in your head that you're a loser, even if you're not aware of it, this soundtrack is going to influence your view of yourself going forward, regardless of your performance or the facts.

Just take any current news story. You have the facts, and then you have the interpretations of the facts. Same facts, two diametrically opposed interpretations based on which channel you listen to. If you drill down, I'm pretty sure you would find that each interpretation is representative of the lived experience of the wider group who espouses it.

So how does this have anything to do with our ability to trust God?

One of the best stories in Scripture to teach us about dealing with our circumstances is the story of Joseph (Genesis 37-50). Joseph is given a spiritual gift to be able to interpret dreams. He is also given a dream about his own life. It's a great dream. He will become the ruler over all his 11 older brothers and the leader of his whole clan. Then his life falls apart.

He's sold into slavery by his jealous brothers, defamed by the governor's wife, unjustly incarcerated, and forgotten by those he helped and who promised to help him. How is it possible that Joseph does not get bitter and curse the Lord?

On the contrary, even amid these horrible circumstances, Joseph maintains his integrity and trust in the Lord. He refuses to do evil in response to his circumstances by giving in to the temptation and seduction of his boss's wife. It would've been so easy and from a human perspective perhaps the way out of his dilemma. His boss, Potiphar the governor, has trusted Joseph with everything in his house. If he became Mrs. Potiphar's boy toy, the chances are she would protect him. But Joseph didn't want her protection. He still trusted the Lord to take care of him and did not want to betray his God or his boss (Genesis 39:9).

Through every circumstance in his life, Joseph chose to trust God. How was he able to do this? **He had to have more than that one-time experience** of the dream God gave him. Scripture tells us that in each situation, God was with Joseph and extended kindness to him at every turn, even in jail (Genesis 39: 2, 21,23). God was with him, providing, protecting, and communicating with him. Joseph continued to have relational experiences with God that reinforced his understanding of God's goodness. **We can know for sure that Joseph did not run away from God in his troubles but rather went to Him.** Joseph had an intimate relationship with the Lord that went beyond the circumstances and allowed him to look at his life through God's perspective: "What you (my brothers) meant for evil God meant for good, to spare you and many people" (Genesis 50:20).

Learning to trust God in difficult situations entails allowing Him to define what we see. Yes, we see "facts" or "circumstances." But it's our perspective on them that determines how we live, react, and interact.

We need to be in a close intimate relationship with the Lord to allow Him to speak to us about His interpretation of our situation. We must be willing to run to Him and not run away from Him in difficult times. We have to trust He is for us and that He knows so much more than we do about what is happening now and will happen in the future (Psalm 56, especially vv. 9-12; Psalm 84, especially vv. 11-12; Psalm 23). As He clearly tells us, "My ways are not your ways" (Isaiah 55:9).

Learning to trust God in difficult situations involves much waiting. I have come to believe that the Lord's favorite word is "wait". It's my least favorite word in the whole English language. Patience has been a struggle my entire life. I'm a type A personality. I need to get things done. I need to check off boxes. But the Lord does not seem to be in a hurry about much.

Jesus portrayed this as He walked about on the earth. We never get a sense of Him being frantic or worried about His time management or reaching quotas. The more I pay attention as I re-read Scripture, the more I see that terrible word, "wait". It's everywhere! The older I get, the more I see this in my lived reality. I'm now 65. My journal of answers to prayer is getting fuller. But all the answers are months if not years in the making.

As I look back at the increasing numbers of answered prayers, I marvel at the goodness and faithfulness of God. I'm ever so slowly beginning to trust as the song goes, "Even when I don't see it, You're working." I'm now sometimes even able to truly "Be still and know that He is

God" (Psalm 46:10). Joseph was an incredible model of this for us.

Through the story of Joseph, God wants us to know that He is bigger than our circumstances. He is for us even when life seems to be against us. He can be trusted with our life and circumstances to redeem and transform even the worst-case scenario **if we will trust Him and stay connected in relationship to Him.** He is good. He is God. And He is for us (Romans 8:28).

2. Fear: The story of the Exodus and the Wilderness

Another common obstacle we experience that makes it difficult for us to trust the Father is fear. **Fear can be about what we know or about what we don't know.** Think about the children of Israel wandering around in the wilderness. I've had the opportunity to walk some of the path they did in the Sinai Peninsula. After doing so, I became much less judgmental of their responses! At the time, I was with my three young kids under the age of ten. I thought about being a young mother in that situation. Certainly, I would have panicked. What am I going to feed my kids? How are they going to be able to walk through this hot, rocky, dry desert? How can I make them new clothes when theirs wear out? How can I protect them from all the perilous snakes and other predators? I would have feared what I did not know. Like the Israelites, I would not have known that God could provide water out of a rock or bring a new kind of bread from heaven no one had ever experienced. **How could God have expected them to trust Him in this situation?**

Psalm 103 is a beautiful answer. The Father is compassionate toward His children and is mindful that we are but dust (vv. 13-14). He knows we are so limited in our understanding of reality. **He is a great master teacher showing us enough to trust for each step. Then He continues to call us deeper, to trust more, and He shows us more of Himself along the way.**

The children of Israel in the desert had heard about the promises God made to their fathers about another land, another inheritance, another destiny they were to have as a people and a great nation (Hebrews 11:23-26). These had to be hard to believe for those who found themselves as the third or fourth generation of slaves. But then, just as He promised, He miraculously frees them from their slavery and the Egyptian lords. They all experienced this. The long-ago promises were becoming true in their very lives. They **saw** the ten plagues the Lord put on the Egyptians and **experienced** the Egyptians letting them go while giving them gold and silver and provisions on their way! Then the Lord parted the Red Sea for them but allowed it to drown their pursuing enemy. Most importantly, He gave them a tangible experience of His presence with them. He would never leave them alone. It was visual. When they doubted, they could simply look to the cloud by day and the fire by night.

How vast was His kindness to them and consideration for their limitations. **They had the promises of the past and the miracles of the present as their foundation of trusting Him for an unknown future.** The more they trusted, the more they saw that He was the God of the impossible. He had power to do things they could not even conceive as possibilities.

Sometimes He leads us into situations where we fear the known, or at least what we have known to this point. The children of Israel who finally made it to the promised land 40 years later had learned that God can be trusted with all the unknowns of how they were going to get through the wilderness. Now it's time to finally conquer and possess the long-awaited promised land. But there's a problem. There are giants in the land! And there are substantially more of them!

This is a new test. In the wilderness, they had to trust God with things they didn't know (like how do you feed 2 million people on a daily basis). Now they are challenged to trust Him with things they do know (giants are bigger and stronger than us, they substantially outnumber us, we cannot beat them).

The Father is calling them deeper, but He has not left them with only wishful thinking to lean on. Moses gathers the whole nation and urges them to remember, in detail, all the miracles the Lord has done for them over these four decades (Deuteronomy 1-11). He tells them, "The Lord your God who goes before you will Himself fight on your behalf, just as He did for you in Egypt **before your eyes**, and in the wilderness where you **saw** how the Lord your God carried you, just as a man carries his son, in all the way you have walked, until you came to this place" (Deuteronomy 1:30-31). **His framework to inspire trust is the same.**

God wants us to remember His promises and all He has done for us. He asks us to trust Him and to follow Him in this new thing. He says, I am bigger than any obstacle in your way and able to remove it if I ask you to face it.

3. Suffering and evil: Jesus and the cross

Perhaps the biggest obstacle to trusting the Lord is the reality of suffering and evil, both in general in the world and specifically in our own lives. This is no small obstacle.

None of us will pass through life without suffering. Pressing into God at these times and not pushing Him away is the fork in the road. If we push Him away in our suffering, we have little hope of finding any meaning in it or redemption of it. We relinquish our ability to receive

His comfort. This will ultimately lead to bitterness and a growing distance from the Lord. You will not be in a position to taste and see His ongoing work in your life, and a downward spiral of a lack of trust will follow.

But pressing into Him in these moments, throwing yourself at His feet, weeping and mourning with Him, wrestling with Him, asking Him all your questions, verbalizing all your anger—and then listening for Him to speak to you—will allow you to grow closer to Him. He will meet you in your darkness and comfort you if you let Him. This will create an upward spiral of experiencing Him showing up for you and a growing ability to trust.

I have observed over the years that those who have pushed the Lord away as a result of their suffering start with comments like, "He could've stopped or healed (this or that), and He didn't." The core issue is that they are extremely angry with Him. In their pain, it is very difficult to embrace that the Lord does not always show up as we want or think He should if He were truly a good God.

I believe it is not possible to sufficiently grapple with this and come to some measure of serenity without deeply immersing yourself in the life and death of Jesus.

For me, the pivotal point is when He is in the Garden of Gethsemane wrestling with the submission of His will to that of the Father's. Hebrews 5:7-8 tells us that Jesus prayed prayers to the Father of loud crying and weeping, prayers of agony and desperation. He prayed these to His Father, the only one able to save His life. And yet His Father allowed Him to go through torture and death.

This is a hard truth to swallow. This reality will turn many away from God. How could a loving Father do this? If you really want to know, you must press into this question and not avoid it. You must read the entirety of the story, contemplate the heart of both the Father and Jesus, and get to the other side of the question to grasp the life-transforming treasures that are waiting for you there. I cannot sufficiently examine this topic here. It is something that takes much individual meditation and study. Many other more gifted authors have written extensively on this topic (see References at the end of the chapter). I offer only a few thoughts.

To become the perfect example for us of what it means to trust the Father, Jesus had to trust Him in the most difficult circumstances imaginable (Hebrews 4:15). **In His humanity, Jesus also had to learn to trust.** How would it have helped us if Jesus lived a life of comfort and ease and then told us, "Trust the Father in all things"? It is only when we see Him trusting His Father to the point of death—and death on a cross—that we step back and say, "Who is this Father that Jesus trusted even in this?"

It is this act of submission of Jesus' will to the Father's that makes us think about the Father's will versus our own. It gives credibility to Jesus when He tells us His Father knows best: "Not my will but Thy will be done" (Luke 22:42).

We must remember that Jesus was one with the Father. He was in eternal intimate communion with Him. The Father's unquestionable, total, and complete love had been Jesus' **experienced reality** for all of eternity. He trusted the Father's love for Him even in suffering. The book of 1 Peter is a necessary study on this topic. Peter tells us that Jesus trusted the Father to be able to accomplish what was right and just even in His suffering and being treated unjustly. Jesus trusted that His Father's goodness, kindness, justice, and love would not be changed by the fact that He was enduring suffering.

In our limited understanding, we believe that it is unloving to not stop someone from suffering if you can. In fact, it is cruel. Of course, there is a continuum of suffering. Most parents would agree there are times where the loving thing to do is to actually allow your children to suffer some. But very few of us, if any, would be able to agree to allow our children to suffer extreme physical pain or death if we could stop it. How would our thinking change if we could know the future? What if we could see the end result of their suffering both in this life and the next?

Unlike us, Jesus saw and knew eternity. He told us that He willingly endured His suffering for the sake of love (John 10:17-18). Additionally, we are told that Jesus endured the pain and humiliation of the cross for the joy that would come as a result (Hebrews 12:2). He knew His death and submission to the Father's will would defeat death for all of humanity and make a way for us all to be able to get back into an intimate, secure relationship with the Father. It would allow the Spirit of God to dwell in man and once again combine the spiritual and physical realms in a real and transforming way, today and not just some day in the distant future. It would allow us to begin to experience eternal life now. The life the Father originally desired for us could be accessed in real ways not known since Adam and Eve through His Spirit living in us.

You might think, "That's all well and good for Jesus. He was the Savior. His suffering saved the world. My suffering is not so grand. It's brutal, and I cannot see any redeeming purpose." Without minimizing your suffering, I want to encourage you that there is a redeeming purpose, though it may not be clear at the moment. The key is to ask the Father for wisdom, understanding, and His interpretation of what is happening or did happen.

The hardest suffering to overcome is that which we experience from the evil of others toward us. I have walked with many people through such suffering. To journey with them to the other side, where they are able to make peace with their reality and learn to trust the Lord and others again, is one of the greatest privileges of my life.

This journey is long and difficult. It can be endured by walking with another. **Suffering is amplified when we suffer alone, and it is bearable when another is present with us to give witness to our suffering and help carry the weight of the shame, pain, anger, and confusion.** Together we bring these to the Lord. We ask Him where He was when this suffering was taking place. The pictures He gives to those who suffer and the things He tells them have been life changing. It has allowed them to trust in His love despite their situation. We have also asked the Father to help them make sense of this suffering and to show them how He will redeem it. It is impossible to move on from suffering until you are able to somehow make sense of it.

Knowing the Father's love and gaining His perspective are the keys to trusting Him amid the suffering and evil in the world. These are the truths repeated to us by those who have gone before us in the faith and echoed throughout Scripture (David in the Psalms, Paul in 2 Corinthians 4, Peter in 1 Peter, Hebrews 11).

I have also seen them lived out by normal people in the here and now. Dick and Donna grappled with the senseless murder of their 16-year-old son at a high school party. Kay and Jerry had to wrestle with their son's suicide. Countless Russian orphans have had to battle with the Lord regarding their histories of abandonment. Vadym and Dima are pressing into the Lord as I write, as they struggle to provide for so many who are suffering the ravages of war in their country of Ukraine.

Yet all of these have chosen to go to the Lord with their severe suffering. They have become witnesses to me of the goodness of God to meet humanity in our darkest nights, bring comfort, and somehow redeem the situations.

I am continually amazed by the deep peace, joy, and sense of purpose they live with. I am humbled as I watch them sincerely worship the God they love. Since we, too, now have access to His Spirit living in us, we can attain this same trust, though not easily. We need to develop resilience in grabbing the hem of His gown and not letting go.

4. Our pride: The story of Saul

The story of King Saul laid out in the book of 1 Samuel is an interesting study. The people of Israel cry to God that they don't want to be ruled exclusively by Him anymore because it's too weird. They want a king they can see and serve, just like all the other nations. God warns them this is not a good idea but says, I'll give you what you want, though you will regret it. God chooses Saul and gives him promises of prosperity and success if he continues to trust and obey the Lord. It doesn't take long for Saul to veer off course.

Despite clear and specific instructions from the Lord for how to rule the nation and engage enemies, Saul decides he will fudge a little bit. He does things the Lord says not to do, does not do things the Lord says to do, and does things from his own mind just because he wants to. He refuses to listen to correction from Samuel, the prophet, but instead tries to bribe the Lord with sacrifices. He is sure he can appease this God in the way the other nations try to appease their gods.

But Yahweh is not like other gods. He is the one and only true God, the maker of heaven and earth. When He gives a command, trusting Him looks like obedience. We trust in His love and wisdom and thus obey what He says. When we choose to lean on our own understanding or will, regardless of what He says, obviously we don't trust Him.

If we are honest with ourselves, sometimes we have difficulty trusting the Lord because we simply don't want to. We just want what we want and don't really care what He says.

Trusting another requires us to assume a position of dependence upon them. Pride assumes the position of

self-sufficiency. Trust or control: they are mutually exclusive polar opposites from which we must choose in each situation. Like Saul, we believe we can do our own thing without suffering any consequences. We live as if God's ways are optional because we do not understand what it means that He is God. We think He is just a little bit bigger than us.

But He is the creator, designer, and owner of everything in heaven and on earth. Like a computer programmer, He knows how the system runs and what commands are necessary to help it function properly. If you choose not to read the instruction manual, you should not be surprised when you crash your computer. Undoubtedly you will be frustrated but you should not be surprised.

I am Exhibit A of such behavior. I always hated taking the time to read instructions and believed I could just figure it out. After a lifetime of dealing with the inevitable consequences and frustration, I have given up this foolishness. Not reading instructions **always** ends up costing me one way or another. Finally, in my older version of myself, I am gaining wisdom. Now I just take a deep breath and sit down to read the directions from whoever made whatever I'm trying to use.

How often do we set aside God's instruction manual, suffer the fallout, and then turn our frustration toward the very One who tried to guide us? When we finally come to our senses and understand Him as God, we may take the next step that Saul did. Once he realized he could not control God, Saul resorted to attempting to bribe Him (1 Samuel 15-16). Saul's thinking is along the lines of, "OK, I messed up, but it really wasn't that big of a deal. We can fix this. Let's just go perform another religious ritual."

But God isn't interested in our rituals. He wants our hearts. He wants us to know Him and His heart toward us that leads us to trust and obedience. Trust says, "I know that you know better. I know you love me and want what's best for me." Pride says, "I know better what's best for me. I'm fully capable of taking care of myself." If this has been our stance in life, simply honestly admitting it to the Lord and "coming clean" is the way forward. A humble "I'm sorry" will allow us to quickly reconcile our relationship with Him.

5. False trust: Not knowing the promises of God

The last obstacle to trusting God I want to explore is not knowing the answer to the question, "What exactly are we to trust the Lord with?" Am I to trust Him with giving me everything I want and ask for? If we do not know what we are told to trust the Lord with, we will ask in vain for many things and be angered at His lack of response to our requests. This makes us vulnerable to the lies of the enemy, like, "See, I told you He doesn't care, isn't listening, etc."

I began asking myself this question a decade ago as I was studying Hebrews 11, the Hall of Fame of believers. I began to see the "assurance" each hero had was simply this: they trusted God to fulfill the specific promises He had given them. Abraham didn't trust God to give him land in Ur, his native country. He trusted God to give him land that He promised, which was in a faraway place. Sarah didn't trust God to give her 1,000 camels (though I think she got those as well). She trusted God to allow her to conceive a child way beyond the normal time of childbearing because that is what He promised her. **Each "hall of famer" had their own unique and specific promises from God and had to trust Him to see them fulfilled.**

David says in Psalm 56:11-12, "In God I have put my trust. I shall not be afraid. What can man do to me? **Thy vows are binding upon me**."

When David wrote this, he was in trouble. The Philistines had seized him and were threatening to kill him. In that dire situation, he prays to God and says, "Hey, Lord, here I am. I'm in trouble. I'm just reminding you that you promised me I would be your king and rule your nation. Your promises (vows) are binding. You have to come through in this situation because you promised my future specifically." It is God's promise to David that allows him to have such trust in this precarious moment.

So what about us? What are the promises of God we are told to trust Him with? This is not an exhaustive list by any means, but it's a good start. I encourage you to add to it.

1. Provision.

Matthew 6:25-34: "Do not be anxious for what you shall eat, or drink, or clothe yourself with. Unbelievers fret about and seek these things, but your Heavenly Father knows that you need them. Seek first His Kingdom, and all these things will be given to you."

2. Protection.

Psalm 121, especially, vv. 7-8: "The Lord will protect you from all evil; He will keep your soul. The Lord will guard your going out and your coming in from this time forth and forever."

Psalm 37, especially v. 40: "The Lord delivers the righteous from the wicked and saves them because they take refuge in Him."

Psalm 91, especially vv. 9-10: "Because you have made the Lord Most High your dwelling place, no evil will befall you."

Psalm 23, especially v. 4: "Even though I walk through the valley of the shadow of death, I will fear no evil for You are with me."

John 17:15: "Father, I do not ask you to take them out of the world, but to keep them from the evil one."

3. His presence.

Matt. 28:20: "I am with you always, even until the end of the age."

John 14:16-23: "I will ask the Father and He will give you another Helper that He may be with you forever, that is the Spirit of truth.... I will not leave you as orphans, I will come to you."

John 17:20-26: "Father, I don't just pray for these disciples but for all who will believe in Me because of their word. I ask you that they may be in Us, just as you are in Me and I am in You.... I ask You, Father, that the love you have for Me would also be in them and I would be in them."

4. His comfort.

Psalm 40:11: "You, Lord, will not withhold your compassion from me, Your lovingkindness and truth will continually preserve me."

Philippians 4:6-8: "Be anxious for nothing, but in all things with prayer and thanksgiving make your requests known to God, and the peace of God which surpasses comprehension will guard your hearts and your minds in Christ Jesus."

1 Peter 5:7: "Cast all your anxiety upon Him because He cares for you."

Matthew 11:28-30: "Come to Me all who are weary and I will give you rest. Take My yoke upon you and learn from Me, for I am gentle and humble in heart and you shall find rest for your souls."

Psalm 23:1-3: "The Lord is my Shepherd, I shall not want. He makes me lie down in green pastures; He leads me besides quiet waters. He restores my soul."

Heb. 4:15-16: "Let us draw near with confidence to the throne of grace, that we may receive mercy and may find grace to help in time of need."

5. His ear, to have a voice with Him.

Matthew 7:7-11: "Ask and it shall be given to you, seek and you shall find; knock and the door shall be opened to you. For everyone who asks, receives…. What man among you will give his son a stone if his son asks him for bread?…If you then, being evil, know how to give good gifts to your children, how much more shall your Father who is in heaven give what is good to those who ask?"

Luke 11:5-8: "Yet because of a man's persistence in prayer, God will give him as much as he needs" (my paraphrase).

James 5:16: "The prayer of a righteous person can accomplish much."

James 4:2: "You do not have because you do not ask."

Matthew 6:6: "When you pray, go into an inner room and shut your door and pray to your Father who is in secret, and your Father who sees in secret will repay you."

Psalm 34:15-17: "The eyes of the Lord are toward the righteous and His ears are open to their cry…. The righteous cry, and the Lord hears and delivers them out of all their troubles."

6. His love.

John 17, the whole chapter.

Ephesians 3:14-19: "I pray that you may be able to comprehend with all believers, what is the breadth, length, height, and depth, to know the love of Christ which passes knowledge."

John 10:10-16: "The thief comes to steal, kill, and destroy. I came to give them life and life abundantly. I am the Good Shepherd; the Good Shepherd lays down His life for the sheep."

Romans 8:35-39: "Who shall separate us from the love of Christ? Shall tribulation or distress, or persecution, famine or nakedness, peril or sword? ... But in all these things we overwhelmingly conquer through Him who loved us. Neither death nor life ... nor any created thing shall be able to separate us from the love of God which is in Christ Jesus our Lord."

7. Good things now.

Psalm 27:13-14: "I would have despaired unless I had believed that I would see the goodness of God in the land of the living."

Psalm 23:6: "Surely goodness and lovingkindness will follow me all days of my life."

Psalm 103:1-5: "Bless the Lord O my soul and forget none of His benefits ... who crowns you with lovingkindness and compassion and who satisfies your years with good things so that your youth is renewed like the eagle."

Psalm 33:18-22: "Let thy lovingkindness be upon us in accordance with how we have hoped in You."

Psalm 34:8-10: "For to those who fear Him there is no want .... Young lions may suffer hunger, but they who seek the Lord shall not be in want of any good thing."

Romans 8:28: "For we know that God causes all things to work together for the good to those who love God and are called according to His purpose."

Psalm 84:11-12: "The Lord God is a sun and a shield; the Lord gives grace and glory. No good thing does He withhold from those who walk with integrity. O Lord of Hosts, how blessed is he who trusts in You."

8. Overcoming death and fear.

Luke 12:4-7: "Are not five sparrows sold for two cents? And yet not one of them is forgotten before God. Indeed, the very hairs of your head are all numbered. Do not fear, you are of more value than many sparrows."

I Thessalonians 5:9-10: "For God has not destined us for wrath, but for obtaining salvation through our Lord Jesus Christ, who died for us, that whether we are awake or asleep, we may live together with Him."

Romans 8:15-16: "For you have not received a spirit of slavery leading to fear again, but you have received a spirit of adoption by which you cry out, 'Abba! Father!' The Spirit Himself bears witness with our spirit that we are children of God."

Romans 8:11: "If the Spirit of Him who raised Jesus from the dead dwells in you, He who raised Christ Jesus from the dead will also give life to your mortal body by His Spirit who dwells in you."

John 11:25-26: "I am the resurrection and the life. He who believes in Me will live even if he dies, and everyone who lives and believes in Me will never die."

2 Timothy 1:7: "For God has not given us a spirit of fear, but of power, love, and a sound mind."

2 Corinthians 5:1-10: "We know that while we are at home in the body we are absent from the Lord ... and we prefer to be absent from the body and at home with the Lord."

1 Corinthians 15, the whole chapter, the assurance of our resurrection.

9. Overcoming evil and having the authority of Christ.

1 John 4:4: "Greater is He who is in you than he who is in the world."

Ephesians 1:18-23: "... which He brought about in Christ when He raised Him from the dead and seated Him in the heavenly places far above all rule and authority, power and dominion not only in this age, but in the age to come. And He put all things in subjection under His feet and gave Him as head over all things to the Church, His body, the fullness of Him who fills all things."

Colossians 2:9-10: "For in Him the fullness of Deity dwells in bodily form, and in Him you have been made complete, and He is the head over all rule and authority."

Revelation 12:10-12: "The accuser of the brethren has been thrown down and the believers overcame him by the blood of the Lamb and the word of their testimony."

Ephesians 6:13-18: "Take up the full armor of God ... in addition to all, take up the shield of faith with which you will be able to extinguish all the flaming missiles of the evil one."

10. His justice.

Luke 18:1-8: "Shall not God bring about justice for His children who cry to Him day and night, will He delay long over them? I tell you that He will bring about justice for them speedily. However, when the Son of Man comes again, will He find faith on the earth?"

11. Blessing to children and grandchildren of those who walk in His ways.

Psalm 103:17-18: "But the lovingkindness of the Lord is from everlasting to everlasting on those who fear Him, and His righteousness to children's children, to those who keep His covenant."

Wow! That's a lot. And there are so many more! If you look closely, you'll see these promises are what's necessary to develop a Secure Attachment.

When we pray according to any of these promises, we can pray like David: "Lord, you said...You promised... You cannot lie...Your vows are binding for me."

Where do you start if you've never started or if you have great difficulty trusting the Lord?

Unlike children who instinctively trust their caregivers because they don't know any different, as adults we don't trust instinctively. We now have enough life experience with those who have hurt us to conclude that trusting others, especially God, might not be a good idea. We have free will and must decide that we want to learn to trust Him.

We must choose to take a step in this direction.

This means to **take a step of dependence upon Him**. Start with something small, like finding an affordable mode of transportation. It might be a used car or access to public transportation. In today's world, this is not a luxury. He knows that. (Maybe this is huge for you. If so, find something else that is a better starting point for you.)

Dare to use your voice. Cry to Him, ask Him. Pray something like, *"Lord, you know I struggle to trust you. I have chosen to try to take care of myself because I'm not confident you really see me or care about the things on my heart. I want to learn to trust you. Your Word tells me to ask you for things I need. It tells me to taste and see that you are good. Help me! I want to trust You with this need of transportation. Please help me find an affordable mode. You know I need it to get to work and to live in this day and age. Please provide this need for me and help me to know that You see me, that You care, that You are for me! Help me to see and hear Your direction and to follow it. Help me to grow in trusting You."*

Then you must listen. Learning to hear His voice is one of the most important life skills we must learn. Here's a simple format I've tried to follow. It's a compilation of things I've learned from others, especially missionary Tom Atwater and author Brad Jersak in his book, *Can You Hear Me? Tuning In to the God Who Speaks*.

a. **Pray**. This is simply talking to God. You don't need to use special "holy" words or change your tone of voice or put on a special pastor's robe. Just come as you are and talk to Him from your heart. Use your normal words. Ask God to help you and to silence the enemy who does NOT want you to hear God. Speak out loud some truths about God that you find in His Word. If you don't know any, start with the promises listed above. *"God, Your Word says You are good. You are the Creator of heaven and earth. You are full of lovingkindness and mercy. You do not turn anyone away who is truly seeking You"* etc. Speaking out loud helps us to focus on what is true, whether we fully believe it yet or not. It encourages us. It changes our perspective.

b. **Read His Word**. The more of His word we have in our minds, the clearer we will be able to hear Him. We will be able to discern His voice from others. We will learn what His voice sounds like (John 10:3,16).

c. **Learn to still your mind**. For most of us, this is the hardest part. This takes discipline and practice. We must grow in learning how to still our mind and not lose heart in the process. I think it is crucial to understand that growing in this skill is a marathon, not a sprint, and to be OK with that.

I adjust a tool from Daniel Siegel in his book *Mindsight*. Find an undistracted place. Sit comfortably and allow your mind to think about a place that is safe and wonderful for you to be at. Just you. It can be real, like your favorite vacation spot. Or it can be imagined, like a beautiful mountain meadow. Thoughts will swirl uncontrollably in your mind. Just let them come and go. Don't grab on to anyone. Try to picture them being carried by the wind, and they just come and go. Focus on imagining Jesus on His throne. Look at His eyes. See if you can settle your mind from all the distracting thoughts and quiet your mind to see and hear the Lord talking to you. Start with doing this for three to five minutes. See if you can increase the time quieting your mind and the time you are able to focus on Jesus. As you practice, this will get easier.

d. **Journal what comes to mind:** thoughts, images, Scripture. Learn to pay attention to what is going on in your mind. The Lord is extremely creative in how He speaks. He uses His Word, His creation, His people, dreams, etc. Not everything we hear is from Him, of course, so we must learn to discern. Is it from Him? From our own minds? The enemy? How do we know? Again, the more of His Word we have in our minds, the less we will be able to be deceived. But it is also important to take one more step.

e. **Ask for confirmation, sit on it, wait.** We can ask, "God, help me to know if this was really from you." I had been asking the Lord for confirmation on some things I thought were from Him but wasn't sure. Five months later, while I was teaching a seminar, I had three attendees come up to me and say, "The Lord wants you to know . . ." All three were clear confirmations of the specific question I was asking the Lord about. Confirmations can come on the same day you ask the Lord, or as in this case, months later.

f. **Step out.** Once you have a sense that "I think this is how God is leading me, what He is telling me," take a step in that direction. As you begin to grow in depending on Him, you will experience His faithfulness. Your ability to trust Him will deepen.

Continue to wrestle with Him. We do not learn to hear His voice and trust Him in a straight line of progress. It's a winding road with many setbacks and twists. The key is to continue to go toward Him in the process and never stop. We must learn to be honest with Him in all our struggles. We can say to Him things like, *"Lord, you said you would come to my rescue. I don't see you. Where are you? I am distraught. I feel like You are not seeing me or caring about my situation."* He honors this kind of prayer. Just check out the Psalms.

Such honest relating to the Lord will allow us to say with David,

"The steps of a man are established by the Lord, and He delights in his way. When he falls, he will not be hurled headlong, because the Lord is the One who holds his hand. I have been young and now I am old, yet I have not seen the righteous forsaken, or his descendants begging for bread. Because the Lord has met his needs, all day long the righteous is gracious and lends, and his descendants are a blessing" (Psalm 37:23-26).

This is not to say that if we trust the Lord and seek Him, our life will be a bed of roses without any suffering or storms, but rather that in all of life we can trust Him. We can trust His love and goodness toward us, so that whatever comes we may be able to say, **and mean it**, "He works all things for good to those who love Him" (Romans 8:28).

CHAPTER 4 MEDITATIONS

Abraham

1. Has God ever told you to do something that made no sense to you? Did you do it or not? What was the result? How did you see God, hear God, experience God in this situation? Would you do things differently going forward?

Joseph

2. What do you assume about God when circumstances are not going your way? About His character? About His power? About His attitude and feelings about you?

3. When times are tough, do you tend to run TO God or away from Him? Who/What do you run to? How do you try to gain control of your circumstances?

4. Do you go to God to listen to His interpretation of your circumstances? If not, why not?

5. Can you identify any childhood experiences of difficult circumstances where you did not feel seen, heard, protected, or provided for?

6. Can you identify any difficult circumstances where you can see God was present and protecting you, providing for you, redeeming things even in the midst of troubles?

Exodus

7. Can you identify current fears of the known? Unknown? What aspect of the Lord's character do you need to be able to trust to give these situations over to Him?

Jesus

8. Have you been able to make sense of your suffering?

9. Have you sensed the Lord meeting you in this suffering?

10. Do you have any sense of how He might want to redeem this?

11. What do you need to say to the Lord about your suffering?

Saul

12. Can you identify areas where your pride has been the real issue in your not trusting the Lord? Can you be honest with the Lord in acknowledging those areas?

Promises

13. Are there any promises of God that were new or surprising to you?

14. What additional promises can you add to the list and share with your group?

15. Are there any things you have expected from God that He has never promised?

Assumptions

16. Can you say like David in Psalm 56:9, "This I know that God is for me"?

If not, how would you fill out this sentence:

"Because if God were for me …<u>this would/would not happen</u>."

How you complete that sentence reveals the assumptions you hold regarding how the Lord should act toward you. This is an important place to meditate. Do our assumptions really expose our impatience? Our narcissism? Desire for MY will and not THY will? Are they in line with what He has promised us?

CHAPTER 4
REFERENCES AND ADDITIONAL READINGS ON SUFFERING

1. *The Broken Way,* by Ann Voskamp (2016)
2. *The Deepest Place,* by Curt Thompson (2023)
3. *Walking with God through Pain and Suffering,* by Timothy Keller (2013)
4. *A Shepherd Looks at Psalm 23,* by W. Phillip Keller (2007)
5. *A Grace Disguised: How the Soul Grows through Loss,* by Jerry Sitser (1995)
6. *What Have You Done Since I Left,* by Donna Mathiowetz (2020)
7. *Finding Meaning: The Sixth Stage of Grief,* by David Kessler (2019)

LEARNING THE PERSONAL NATURE OF GOD THROUGH EXPERIENCES

I Know You, I See You

Often when I read Scripture, I find my heart simultaneously filled with both longing and frustration. My conversations with the Lord frequently lament things like, "Lord, if you showed up for me in a burning bush, I could be like Moses!" I believe with all my being that the deepest yearning of every human heart is to be seen and known and loved as a unique individual, foremost by our Creator and our parents. At our core, we do not want collective promises. We want individual promises. I want the Lord to talk to me, Melinda, not us. I want to know He sees MY situation and cares. I need Him to touch MY heart.

As babies, we come into the world clueless about who we are. We look toward our parents' faces to learn the answer. Babies are designed to be glued to these faces; the eyes, the smiles, the tones of the voices. These are our first mirrors through which we see ourselves. What do we see there? When we see and hear joy and delight, we become filled with the same. When we are attended to in such a way that we feel **seen** (our whole being, physically and emotionally), **known** (understood in our uniqueness and our situations), and **loved**; we are full. **It is only when we are in this satiated condition that we can truly think of others**. It is an irony. We tend to think of narcissists as self-absorbed. They are. But I believe very often it is because they are empty inside. When you are empty, you must focus on yourself so you don't die. It's only when you are full that you don't need to pay attention to yourself and you are able to look to and care for others.

God also wants us to experience this with Him. How often in His word does He encourage us to seek HIS FACE?

"You have said, 'Seek My face.' Your face, O Lord, I will seek" (Psalm 27:8).

I love the blessing He told Moses and Aaron to speak over the Israelites.

The Lord bless you and keep you. The Lord make **His face shine** *upon You and be gracious to you; The Lord lift up* **His countenance upon you** *and give you peace"*

(Numbers 6:23-27).

I am convinced that if we were able to see His face upon us, with all the love and delight He has toward us, all our troubles would melt away. Like the words of the old hymn, "Turn your eyes upon Jesus. Look full in His wonderful face, and the things of earth will grow strangely dim in the light of His glory and grace."

He has given us so many examples in Scripture to encourage us to do just that. Let's look at a few.

Hagar

The first story that comes to mind is the story of Hagar. I love that it is told to us so early in the Scriptures. Clearly, this is an important theme the Lord wants us to know early on (Genesis 16).

As a foreign teenage slave, Hagar is a nobody. She is a piece of property. She has very little, if any, power or rights. Day in and day out, she simply does what she's told. It's difficult for most of us to comprehend the depth of powerlessness and lack of dignity she must have experienced.

When she's forced to have her boss's (Abraham's) baby, she then experiences more indignity. The jealous wife (Sarah), who created this mess in the first place, begins to mistreat her. Abraham doesn't care about her and tells Sarah, "She's your slave, do what you want to her" (Genesis 16:6).

So Sarah treats her worse.

Scared, alone with an unwanted pregnancy, she runs away in the wilderness. What is Hagar to do? Who cares about HER? Who sees HER? The Lord comes to her and gives her a plan that will take care of her during her pregnancy. He tells her to go back and promises that He will watch out for her. Furthermore, her son, whom Sarah would despise, God promised to bless.

Hagar is blown away. She has learned and proclaims, "I have seen God and I know He sees ME. He knows my situation and is for ME!" (Genesis 16:13, my paraphrase).

Hagar trusts God and returns. In her experience with God, she comes to know His individual love and care for her and calls Him "the God who sees" (Genesis 16:13).

The Woman at the Well

One normal day, an unsuspecting woman is just going about her daily chores when she has an encounter with Jesus. She can tell he's a foreigner in her parts, and from a tribe with which her people have a lot of animosity. In the course of their conversation, Jesus informs her that He knows her current situation and her sin. She's living with her fifth man who is not her husband. Her response is what is so revealing to me. She's excited! She's so excited that she runs back to town to tell everyone about this man. That's not how I respond when my sin is exposed! I bet it's not your response either. What's going on? What could explain this kind of response? I think it's the fact that she felt SEEN and KNOWN by Jesus.

In that culture and time, it was very unusual for a woman to not be married. To have had five live-in boy-friends and no husband tells us she must not have been very wanted or valued for who she was. Maybe she was particularly ugly. But this man (Jesus) is even willing to break cultural norms to talk to her and convince her that He SAW HER and KNEW HER. She had to feel special.

But not only did He see her, He related to her with shocking kindness and love. Instead of the normal cultural response of judgment and rejection, He offered her eternal life and revealed that He was the Messiah. This is not a "I'll strike you with lightning" god way out in the cosmos somewhere. This is a personal God who came to her in her individual life and situation to convince her that He sees her and that He cares. He earned her trust and love. She cannot help but share her joy with everyone she knows. As she tells her testimony, the townspeople are so in-trigued they must come and see for themselves. This is what happens when we experience being seen, known, and loved: We feel peace and joy and are compelled to share about our lover or friend with others (John 4:7-42).

Doubting Thomas

I think we can probably all relate to the disciple, Thomas, who would not believe the others' accounts of Jesus' resurrection. They claimed to have seen the risen Lord. Thomas was not present for this amazing miracle. But he was present for the crucifixion. In that moment, his whole life had blown apart. All his hopes and dreams for the future were dashed. Everything he thought he knew or had learned—about God, Israel, his own future—was apparently a lie. So much for Jesus being the Son of God!

He was not believing this hype anymore. He would not believe anything short of seeing the risen Christ with his own eyes and touching the holes in Jesus' hands with his own hands.

Jesus heard Thomas say this, and so the next time He shows up, He makes sure it's when Thomas is present. He goes right up to Thomas and says, "Look Thomas, it's Me. See my holes, touch my wounds" (John 20:19-31, my paraphrase).

Jesus saw Thomas in his hour of greatest despair. He came to him in exactly the way Thomas needed and in response to the deepest cry of his heart. Thomas responds with utter shock and complete trust. My God is alive, and HE SEES ME and HEARS ME and CARES FOR ME!

Jesus earned Thomas' trust and worship, which were deep enough for Thomas to endure being martyred for His name. Having a personal encounter with Jesus and knowing His individual love for us is essential to living a faithful life until the end.

Zacchaeus

Zacchaeus was a despised traitor in his culture. Being a tax collector meant being corrupt and oppressive toward your own people. Clearly his aim was money and power. Zacchaeus was also very short. We can surmise he had some kind of Napoleonic complex, compensating for his physical insecurity by his financial status and power.

Yet something about Jesus was so intriguing that Zacchaeus climbs a tree just to get a glimpse of Him passing by on the road. And Jesus SEES HIM. Jesus sees the real Zacchaeus, the insecure Zacchaeus and all the longings of his heart. Jesus calls Zacchaeus to come down and meet Him. He further invites Himself to Zacchaeus' house for dinner. He is not afraid to be seen with Zacchaeus or have dinner with all his corrupt friends. Jesus risks scandal by doing this publicly. The fact that Jesus SAW Zacchaeus for who he really was and met his deepest need for belonging and acceptance led Zacchaeus to trust Jesus and repent of all his theft and extortions. He clearly learned to be secure in Jesus' love instead of needing to create a false sense of security for himself. This is what happens when we experience being SEEN and LOVED by our Creator to the core. We become secure and able to live in love toward others (Luke 19:2-8).

These are just a few of the many stories throughout all Scripture that flesh out Psalm 139.

"O Lord, you have searched me and known me. You know when I sit down and when I rise. You understand all my thoughts. … You are intimately acquainted with all my ways. Before I speak any word, You already know what I will say. … You formed all my inward parts when you wove me in my mother's womb. … Your eyes have seen my unformed substance, and in Your book were written all the days that were ordained for me before there was even one of them."

These stories are not meant to be just for these individuals of long ago. They are meant to show us the heart of our Father, that He is a Father who sees and knows His children individually, and to encourage us also to seek His face in our lives with confidence in His love for us. I have many firsthand testimonies of God doing the same for normal people today. And I have many testimonies in my own life. One such occasion is embarrassing to tell. I only do so to testify to the extravagant love of our Father.

When we moved back to the U.S. from Russia, we moved to an affluent suburb of St. Paul, Minnesota. Our kids went to an expensive private school we could only afford because of donors and extreme missionary discounts. They received free lunches, and we had government health care. Our oldest daughter, Danielle, was confused. One day she asked, "Mom, are we rich or are we poor?" What an opportunity to talk about life values. I told her, "It depends on your reference point doesn't it? In Russia we are rich. In the U.S. we are poor. But in the things that matter, we are truly rich." A great sermon that I didn't fully believe myself. Internally, I was jealous of all the material things our new friends had and opportunities they could afford to give their kids. I was feeling particularly sorry for myself one year and complaining to the Lord about not being able to provide such opportunities for our kids. I sensed Him telling me to ask Him concretely and specifically for what I wanted. It was a ridiculous desire, especially given the situations of most of the poor people I worked with. Again, I sensed Him urging me to ask Him, so I did. Sheepishly, I told the Lord I wanted Mark and I to be able to take our children on a ski vacation in Colorado. I kid you not. The next week, an acquaintance called me out of the blue. She and her husband felt led to offer us to join their family on a ski vacation in Colorado!! They would pay for everything except our gas to get there.

I was speechless. It was a dream come true. I knew without a doubt that God saw me, heard me and was willing to meet even this ridiculous request just to say, "See how much I love you and your family? Trust Me." I knew His answer had nothing to do with my being worthy, but everything to do with His desire to prove His love.

Though He designed us to be in loving community with each other as humans, we cannot look to them to get our soul full. Only our Heavenly Father, our source of life, the source of love, can fill us so we are full.

Chapter 5 Meditations

1. Can you relate to any of these four stories? Which one do you relate most to?

2. Have you ever had an experience with Jesus where you knew He saw YOU and heard YOU? What was that like? How has it continued to impact you? Your confidence in Him?

3. How would you like Jesus to meet you in your life now? What would you like Him to SEE about your heart, your situation? What are the cries of your heart you would like Him to HEAR?

4. Can you ask Him to meet you in these places?

5. If you have not experienced any such encounters with Jesus, why do you think you have not?
   - You don't believe He will?
   - You don't believe He wants to?
   - You don't believe He can?
   - You have never asked?
   - You have never looked at or thought about ways He has been there for you throughout your life?
   - You believe you are too much of a sinner or too damaged?

6. Consider again the people in the above stories. Put yourself in their shoes. Ask God to speak to you about how He feels about YOU. Go back to the

promises of God and see which promises you are not believing. Dare to ask Him to meet YOU and let you know that He sees YOU.

SECTION 3

HEALING WITH HUMANITY

DEVELOPING EARNED SECURITY AND LEARNING TO TRUST OTHERS

In summary, trust is foundational to all relationships, with people and with God. We first learn to trust (or not) in our relationship with our primary caregivers. We transfer the style of relating we develop with them onto our relationship with God and others. Whatever style we learn **becomes the model for how we develop and navigate future relationships**.

Additionally, what we learn about the world and ourselves in this first relationship **creates a set of lenses through which we see, understand, and interpret our identity, current circumstances, and reality.** This learned pattern creates feedback loops of self-fulfilling prophecies. This is good news if you have a secure attachment style.

But what if you don't? Without awareness and intentionality to change, we will continue to live in and recreate insecure/dysfunctional patterns of relating that destroy trust and inhibit the ability to have deeply intimate, loving, life-giving relationships.

Thankfully, change is possible. It is possible to learn to trust others. We can actually rewire our brains and change our DNA and what we pass on to future generations. (For more on this, read up on the field of epigenetics.) I have witnessed dozens of orphans, neglected and abandoned, who have learned to trust. Some have gone from being sex trafficked and living on the streets to having stable marriages going on twenty years. I have seen the beautiful transformation in their lives as they parent their own children and choose to break the cycle they were born into.

This intentionality to change is not quick or easy. Developing new lenses and new patterns is a journey that requires time and energy. Thus, the term "Earned-Secure" has been coined by experts to describe the style of attachment that's possible for each of us to earn by our hard work. Let's review the attachment styles and then consider steps to take to develop an Earned-Secure attachment.

If I have a **Secure Attachment style**, my needs were met by my primary caregiver in adequate, predictable, and emotionally nurturing ways. Thus, I believe I am loved, the world is basically safe, and I can trust others. When I read the Bible, I will understand God through this lens. Of course, He loves me and can be trusted. When I come upon difficult times, I don't run away from God; I run to Him and feel confident in sharing my anxieties with Him. I will do the same with others. I will go to them when I need comfort because I possess the four qualities of a Secure Attachment; I can give nurture, receive nurture, use my voice to negotiate my needs, and have a stable sense of my identity. I connect with God and others in a secure way, developing intimacy that reinforces my secure attachment. "Yes, I am loved. God and others can be trusted."

However, if I have an **Avoidant Attachment style**, my primary caregiver was unable to meet my needs on an emotional level. Therefore, I don't trust people with my emotional life. I don't trust God with it either. In difficult times, I won't run to God but instead do what I do in human relationships: isolate and deal with my anxieties on my own. This usually involves some type of distraction, healthy (exercise) or unhealthy (eating or drinking).

The emotionally compromised lens I wear makes it difficult to see the emotional side of God throughout the Bible. I ignore, minimize, or filter that out. I see and understand God as only being concerned about my behavior and relating to me on that level. I don't think others care about my deep inner being either, so I never go there with anyone. In fact, I have learned to not even pay attention to this part of me. In relating to Him and others on primarily a task or activity level, deep intimacy and a feeling of being truly seen and known are missing. This, too, will reinforce my lens that God and others cannot be trusted with my emotions.

If my attachment style is an **Ambivalent Attachment**, my primary caregiver was unable to meet my needs predictably. So, I struggle with trusting that people will be there for me consistently. With God, I tend to have a relationship that is characterized by striving or trying to bribe Him with good works. Like the pagans of old, I will think about what I need to do to appease this god and get into His good graces so He will do what I want or need. When this doesn't work, or when I'm afraid of His rejection, I will push away. This push/pull is the hallmark of an Ambivalent style.

It's similar in my relationships with people. I'm not confident that they will predictably be there for me. This fear leads me to try to control the relationship. Control might look like manipulation. Or it might look like being very needy and clingy in an attempt to keep them close to me. Or it could look like being very whiny and dramatic. Anything to keep their focus on me and not leave me.

Of course, the irony is that these behaviors push people away. The constant push/pull is confusing and exhausting for those in such relationships. The very thing Ambivalent styles fear, unpredictability in relationships, is what they create.

Lastly, if I struggle with a **Disorganized Attachment style**, my primary caregiver was absent, neglectful, or threatening in some way. I will have no sense of who I am nor any coherent strategy for how to function in the world or relationships. In this situation, it would be unlikely I would pursue a relationship with God in any consistent way. I may "give religion a try" but quickly discard it when I'm not able to reach God. Similarly, I would tend to have serial chaotic relationships with people. I may dive headfirst into a dysfunctional relationship, stay in it too long, and then leave. This pattern would be repeated many times. I live a lot of my life being "zoned out," unconnected from myself, others, and God.

Learning to trust others

As we discussed in Chapter 4, learning to trust takes corrective experiences. It bears repeating: trust must be earned. We are predisposed as infants to trust our caregivers. If we did not trust them, it is because they were not worthy of our trust: unavailable emotionally, unpredictable, neglectful, or abusive. To reverse this requires being in relationships that will give us different experiences, ones that earn our trust. This is easier said than done, of course. How do you find or develop such relationships? Below are some suggestions to start. **This is not a comprehensive list, but rather some suggestions** I and others have found helpful.

Proactive work:

All relationships involve two parties. If we want to learn to develop healthy trusting relationships, we need to be aware of how we typically show up and what biases we have that create obstacles. We need to be willing to change our lenses. As we have seen, our experiences create lenses that determine how we **interpret the present** and **anticipate the future**. They inhibit us from seeing "objective reality." These become our biases. We all have them, which creates many problems in developing trusting relationships.

For example, if I have an Avoidant Attachment style and my experience is that people do not see me or attend to my emotional needs, when I try to tell you about a hurt I'm experiencing in a work relationship and you're busy checking your phone or don't seem present to me, I get angry. I will shut down or lash out at you. I'm unable to see or consider that my timing in telling you my story was not good for you. You're dealing with a crisis of your own.

There are so many situations where what we're fighting about is not the issue. The issue is how YOU interpret the interaction (your lens) versus how I interpret the interaction (my lens). It's about how this current interaction is triggering both your old wounds and mine. **If we are not aware of how we contribute to this mess, it will be very difficult to find or develop corrective trusting relationships**. This is where we need to start, dealing with our own stuff.

1. Develop awareness.

There are many things we must become aware of in our journey of growth into an Earned-Secure attachment.

a. **What is your attachment style?** To the best of your ability, determine what it is. Think about the four characteristics of a Secure Attachment. Which ones do you possess? Of the parenting styles described in Chapters 1 and 3, which ones best fit your childhood that you can remember? Ask an older sibling or extended family member to gain a fuller perspective on your recollections. Look at your current relationships and honestly assess what consistent obstacles you encounter. Do you struggle with emotional intimacy, for example? That is a clue you have an Avoidant Attachment style. Look back at the obstacles listed for each style to help you think about this.

b. You may have a combination of styles. Often people have some characteristics of Avoidant and some of Ambivalent. That's OK. You just have to deal with the issues of both. Also, keep in mind that you will develop a unique style with each parent or caregiver who consistently raised you in the first three years. They might be the same or different. For example, if you had two parents and a nanny, you might have experienced a Secure Attachment with one and Ambivalent Attachments with two. **The important thing is to become aware of how your childhood impacted the way you understand and navigate relationships now.**

c. **What messages of Felt-Safety did you receive/not receive from your primary caregivers?** (I see you, I hear you, I will protect you, I will meet your needs, I will be with you/not abandon you, I will comfort you, I will delight in you.) How did this form your identity? What messages do you struggle with receiving from others?

d. **What lenses do you wear regarding your identity and the world?** (Are you loved, worthy, valued? Is the world safe, trustworthy, predictable?)

e. **How do your lenses cause you to understand and interpret your current circumstances?** For example, if there is silence in a group setting, do you think (usually subconsciously):

- "No one likes me. I'm invisible." You feel really insecure. You try to avoid connecting. You do something to try to soothe your discomfort (distract yourself, look at your phone, etc.). – Avoidant style

- "I'm not being validated if people are not paying attention to me. I need to get their attention to be noticed and validated. I need to tell a joke or do something to get attention." – Ambivalent style

- "I don't know what's going on. I just need to disappear." You zone out or maybe physically leave. – Disorganized style

- "People are probably busy thinking about the question, or maybe they are simply self-absorbed thinking about their lives. Their behavior is about them, not me." You can be secure in the silence and present. – Secure style

f. **How do your lenses cause you to anticipate the future?** Are you a glass half full or glass half empty person? Do you think (usually subconsciously):

- "I'm on my own. I better do whatever it takes to take care of myself. People cannot be trusted with my emotional/internal life." You live with a sense of loneliness and have tendencies toward depression and anxiety. – Avoidant style
- "The future is unpredictable and random. I need to try to do what I can to control it." You have tendencies toward anger, fear, and anxiety. – Ambivalent style
- "Life is chaotic. There is no potential to make any sense of it. I'm completely helpless. I need to dissociate from the present and reality." You have tendencies toward dissociative disorders, personality disorders, depression, and substance abuse. – Disorganized style
- "I have the ability to make something out of my life. I have agency/power to get my needs met. I know how to find people to help me. Life and the future are good." You have tendencies toward hope, joy, and peace. – Secure style

g. **Think about and list those who have significantly wounded you in the past.** Even though these are not your primary caregivers, wounds we receive later on in significant relationships can hugely impact our identities and our ability to trust others going forward. My experience sitting with others as a counselor for almost 40 years is that most of us have experienced deep and long-lasting wounds in elementary and middle school, as well as in early romantic relationships. Think about who wounded you. How did they wound you? What messages about yourself and the world did you learn from that experience? What vows did you make as a result of that? How has it impacted your life and relationships going forward?

h. **List specific areas of growth to intentionally pursue.** You can't change many things at once. Identify two or three areas you want to grow in. As you progress in those areas, add new ones. Consider these areas:

- Learn to use your voice, ask for what you want or need.
- Learn to negotiate your needs and compromise.
- Have courage to not run away from emotional conversations.
- Learn to go to a significant other for comfort.
- Grow in trying to become aware of and value others' emotional lives.
- Be OK with not being OK with emotions (yours and others'), give yourself grace to learn how to just let them be.

- Try to be less controlling; just ask for what you want or need; allow others to have their own opinions, ways of doing things, etc.
- Learn to be a listener and not have to fix problems.
- Grow in ability to give nurture and affection to others.
- Grow in ability to receive nurture and affection from others.
- Grow in knowing your identity in Christ and how He has uniquely made you.
- Grow in being stable in your identity in various contexts, not a chameleon.
- Grow in ability to be comfortable being alone.
- Grow in intentionally taking time to do self-evaluations and asking for feedback from a few trusted friends.
- Grow in ability to be present, not mentally distracted or checked out.
- Grow in understanding your lenses and how they create obstacles in relationships.
- Grow in your willingness to let go of your lenses.
- There are many others. Share with your group others you have come up with.

i. **Develop an emotional vocabulary.** Most of us have a woefully insufficient emotional vocabulary, not just those with an Avoidant Attachment style. If we are going to develop trusting relationships, emotions are a significant part of that. It is necessary to communicate to others not only what we think, but also what we feel. This allows them to connect with our deepest parts. It allows them to more fully see and understand us. All our thoughts have corresponding emotions. It is impossible to think without feeling. You might not be aware of the feelings, but they are present as electrochemical messages flowing through your brain and body. **What feeling you have is dependent on how you interpret the situation or sensations you are experiencing**. If you are afraid of dogs, the presence of a big black lab running toward you will elicit fear and release stress neurotransmitters. This happens whether you are aware of it or not. On the other hand, if you have had positive experiences with dogs, the big black lab running toward you will elicit pleasurable neurotransmitters and you will relish in him jumping on you to play

If I am the dog-lover and you are terrified of dogs, and we are just beginning to develop a relationship and don't understand this about each other, things might go awry.

If I see you respond to my black lab with an angry voice or using your leg to kick him away, this will be an obstacle in our developing a further relationship. However, if you tell me, "I'm really afraid of dogs. I got attacked by one when I was little," it changes the whole experience for me. Now I have an understanding of your internal world. I'm able to have empathy, and maybe I will kennel my dog when we get together. Your behavior is no longer an obstacle for me wanting to develop a deeper relationship with you.

We are body, soul, and spirit. To develop rich, trusting relationships, we want someone to relate to all of us, not just our head. We need to learn to communicate clearly what we are feeling. There are many simple "emotion wheels" easily accessible online that can help you grow in identifying different emotions. Find one you like and learn an emotional vocabulary.

> j.   **Tune into your body.** For me, this has been a huge learning curve in pursuing my personal growth. Being a therapist, I understood the importance of emotions and the necessity of learning an emotional vocabulary. I was also aware of how bad I was at this. It wasn't until I learned TBRI that I began to understand the role my body played in being able to identify my emotions and the importance of paying attention to them for my

overall emotional, relational, spiritual, and physical health.

Being raised by an emotionally unavailable mother due to her own trauma, I learned to not pay attention to my own emotions. Apparently, they were not important, and they were certainly not going to be attended to—whether by comfort, empathy, or delight. I shut down emotionally. That part of my brain was underdeveloped, which an MRI would have shown in decreased electrical activity and neurological connections in that area. I did not learn emotional vocabulary since it was not used in my relationships. Nevertheless, emotions were alive and well in me and brimming below the surface. As I mentioned in the previous section, just because we are unaware of our emotions does not mean they are absent. All this emotional energy bubbling underneath would explode out of nowhere. It drove many embarrassing behaviors. Some may argue, "This is too much attention on emotions. I don't want to focus on them and have them rule me." The irony is that it's when we don't pay attention to them that they have the power to control us. We are only able to control that which we are aware of.

I had to learn to become aware of all those emotions that were alive within me under the surface. The problem was how to access them. To do this, I had to learn to tune into my body. It's easy to deceive our minds. It's much harder to deceive our body. Tuning into it can tell us what we really feel. If I have a knot in my stomach and begin to pay attention to it and ask myself, "What is this about?," I will realize that I'm feeling anxious about an upcoming public speaking event or interview. Now I have information to help me choose what to do about these emotions. Do I need to review my notes? Do I need to take a walk? Without this attuned information, my stomach will continue to be in knots. I might have increased anxiety being afraid I'll have to go to the bathroom in the middle of my speech or interview. In extreme circumstances, I might even feign sickness to have an excuse to miss having to perform either of these tasks. Our bodies are constantly giving us important information that we need to learn to pay attention to in order to better navigate our own lives and relationships.

Here are two simple ways to tune in:

Body Mapping

This is an effective tool used by many therapists. Simply draw a stick figure. Use whatever color of marker you want to indicate what you are feeling and draw it on the figure. Label it with the name of the emotion, such as angry, anxious, or in love. Where is it located in your body?

How big, how heavy is it? What shape is it?

What color would you use to express it?

Angry   Anxious   In Love

There are no right and wrong answers. It's your perception, and you're just trying to increase your awareness. When I initially do this with clients, they think it's very childish and are somewhat resistant. However, once they begin to do it, they use it often on their own. It creates awareness of what you're feeling and understanding of why you may be having those awful headaches or heartburn, for example. It forces you to pay attention to what's going on inside your body and get it down on paper so you can look at it and make informed decisions about what you need to do. If you struggle to identify and name emotions, simply google "feeling wheel" and you will find many resources to help.

Body Scans

This is another tool used by many therapists. I learned it from Daniel Siegel in his book *Mindsight*.

Find a place of quiet and minimal distraction. Place your feet on the floor, close your eyes and take a few deep breaths. Use your mind's eye to do a scan or X-ray over your whole body. Focus on each point for ten to fifteen seconds: head, eyes, jaw, neck, shoulders, upper back, arms, middle back, lower back, stomach, hips, thighs, knees, lower legs, and feet. Where is there pain or tightness? Can you relate it to anything like a looming deadline or financial worries? Name the feelings associated with it. (Note: Siegel has a phrase he uses, "**Name it to tame it**," to help us remember that simply naming our emotions *accurately and specifically* releases a calming neurotransmitter in our brains.) Our brains will not release calming neurotransmitters if we use general terms. So, if we identify a knot in our stomach and tell ourselves we feel "bad", there may not be any sense of calming. However, if we say, "I am anxious, or afraid" our brains and bodies will calm down. By looking at a list of emotional words and synonyms, we will be able to identify which word is the accurate one in our current situation.

Naming our emotions out loud signals to our body that it is seen and understood and allows it to calm down. There is a large amount of research behind these findings. Whether you can name the emotions or not, try to relax and stretch the tight places. If there is pain, try rubbing it.

If you consistently use these two simple tools, your awareness of what is going on inside you will dramatically increase. It will help you make sense of some of your thoughts, feelings, and behaviors. It will also help you understand your physical conditions better. **If we want to develop trusting relationships, we need to grow in awareness of ourselves so that we can better communicate with others and have control and choice over our own actions and responses.**

One last comment on our body: I think it's important to understand how emotions impact it. I like to think of emotions as electrical motion. As mentioned above, **emotions have physical expressions in our brains and bodies in the form of electrical pulses and chemical neurotransmitters.** The purpose of emotions is to move us, to propel us to some kind of action. Joy and excitement are supposed to move us to sing and dance and laugh. Sadness is designed to move us to cry and find someone to hug. Fear should move us to run or fight. Love propels us to sacrifice. When emotions are not expressed, they get stuck in the body. The electrical pulses and neurotransmitters build up much like pus in an infected wound. Much research correlates stuck or unexpressed emotions with many chronic health issues. (For a deeper dive, check out Dr. Nadine Burke Harris' TED talk on ACEs) **Our emotions simply will not be ignored. The more we try to silence them, the louder they scream**. Paying attention to our body is crucial to being able to figure out how to constructively express our emotions and develop trusting relationships. The seminal book on this topic is *The Body Keeps the Score* by Bessel A. van der Kolk.

Know how your brain works. Turn your relational Wi-Fi on. This week I've been battling with my phone. The connection has been horrible. Calls dropped. I had intermittent internet. I checked the new router. I went to the phone store twice to have them check my phone. I checked the battery. Nothing. No explanation. As I was looking at my control panel for something else, I noticed my Wi-Fi was not on! I switched it on, and all my connection issues were immediately resolved.

Our brain works very much like this. Our brain can be "on" and receptive to connection or "off" and closed to connection. It cannot be both. The "on" brain functions out of the frontal cortex, the uniquely human part of the brain designed by God for connection. No other animal has a frontal cortex like ours that can connect with others like we do. This is the part of the brain we use for reasoning, language, empathy, moral judgments, attachment, decision-making, and all other higher functioning. The "off" brain utilizes the survival brain that is instinctive. When we function out of this part of the brain, we will automatically respond defensively or in a reactive, impulsive manner. We're not able to be present and attuned to the person in front of us. It's designed for our protection in moments of crises and threat. Such situations call for quick responses, not thinking, for example if your house is on fire. So, your brain shuts off access to the frontal cortex to eliminate this possibility. No time for connecting. It's time to fight, flee, or freeze.

Although fear of a perceived threat is the primary thing that shuts off our Wi-Fi, other intense emotions will do the same thing. Rage or resentment also turn off receptivity to connection. Have you ever been in an argument with someone who simply cannot listen to you because they are so angry? It's actually neurologically impossible for them to do so. For us to be open and receptive to connection, our Wi-Fi must be turned on. This will only happen if our survival brain is calmed. Our brain calms when there is no longer a perceived threat (physical or emotional) or when anger and rage have subsided.

When we want to connect with others, we need to remember to check our Wi-Fi. Is our brain in an "on" or "off" position? Are we open and receptive to connecting, or are we in an agitated or fearful state? I may want to connect with my spouse but be very upset about a situation at work. I need to be aware and do whatever I need to do to calm my brain and get to an "on" state.

If I'm in a situation that becomes very heated and triggers my old wounds, I need to learn to step away for several minutes or even hours until I can get myself in a position to turn the connecting brain back "on". It's pointless to attempt any connecting or reasonable communication when my brain is in the "off" position.

This is also why it's so important to resolve conflicts as quickly as possible. The Lord's command to "not let the sun go down on our anger" (Ephesians 4:26) reflects His knowledge of our brains! His loving direction is meant to keep us and our relationships healthy. Unresolved conflicts leave open wounds that are easily triggered. When such a wound is triggered in a new argument, the brain perceives it as a current threat and shuts down. If one or both parties are in their "off" brain, it's impossible to be reasonable and heal these old wounds. Both need to be in their calm "on" brain. Getting there can be difficult, but there is no other path to developing trusting connections.

Frontal Cortex		Limbic Area & Brain Stem
"Off"- unavailable for connection or usage of higher functions	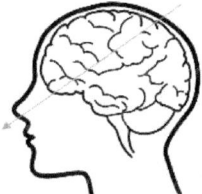	Fight, Flight & Freeze, responds instinctually to threats (real or perceived)
		Not open for connection, but for survival

Frontal Cortex		Limbic Area & Brain Stem
"On" - available for connection & usage of higher functions	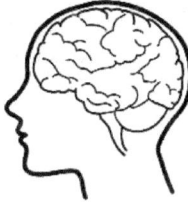	Threat is gone. Felt-safety has been achieved.
Place of calm and felt-safety		

Develop connections.

After all that work on ourselves, eventually we need to begin to develop connections with others. For some people, this is easy. For others, the thought of diving into truly intimate trusting relationships is daunting. Most of us would agree that our current U.S. population suffers an epidemic of loneliness and isolation. Surrounded by many acquaintances and receiving lots of social media "likes" doesn't satisfy the soul's deepest longing to be seen, known, and loved in trusting relationships. Meaningful connections are missing. This is why anxiety and depression are so prevalent today.

If knowing how to break through your angst to pursue meaningful relationships is difficult for you, I offer these recommendations:

Start by using your voice.
If you're going to have a trusting relationship with someone, they need to be able to hear you, so they understand your wants and needs. They will have to respect your boundaries and be able to negotiate your needs with you. Whether you're developing a new relationship or going deeper in an old one, start by using your voice with them in a more honest way. Talk clearly about your thoughts, feelings, wants, needs, dreams, fears, and boundaries. See how they respond.

If this is new for you, you might be tempted to go all-in and dive straight into the deep end. Doing so is unwise if you have not tested their trustworthiness. It is also overwhelming to them and may create unwanted responses from them like shutting down or avoiding you.

Share small things that are just a little bit vulnerable. If they hear you, share more. If they're not able to hear you or respect you, you probably won't and shouldn't share more vulnerably. Ask the Lord to bring good friends and deep relationships in your life. You're most likely to find them with those who have similar interests. Keep testing the waters, and you'll find those with whom you can go deeper.

Find ways to "play" together.
Playing together is the fastest way to bond. This is true for both children and adults. A round of golf, eating out, going to a show, watching a ball game, gardening together can create fun, informal, safe environments that are the soil in which rich conversations and deeper relationships develop.

Become dependent.
Yes, you read that correctly! Remember, we can only learn to trust if we are dependent on someone. This is where many of us quit and why most of us have only acquaintances. If we don't need them, why do we need to trust them? Again, start small. Find something you need from this relationship. Everyone wants to be needed. Maybe it's relying on them for new recipes. Or maybe they can show you how to build a tree house for your children or help you learn to change the oil in your car.

I learned the importance of this in 1992 when I moved to St. Petersburg, Russia, as a missionary. I became dependent on my Russian acquaintances out of sheer necessity. The culture was so different. I had no clue how to shop for groceries or navigate public transportation, especially with a toddler. My Russian language skills were the worst on our team at the time. Surprisingly, my need for them endeared me to them and quickened the development of deep, intimate relationships. It took me a while to understand this, but eventually I got it. My dependence on them put me in a position of humility. I was not the know-it-all missionary who came with all the answers. They had much to offer me, more in fact than I had to offer them. This allowed for a more mutual relationship to develop. I learned to trust them deeply. Reciprocally, they learned to trust me deeply as they saw how I responded to them.

Obviously, there is a continuum of how dependent we should be on others. We are talking about learning to develop deep, trusting relationships. In these situations, I'm suggesting we find some degree of dependence that will allow us to have a mutual relationship. We need to refrain from overwhelming them or expecting things that others are not willing or able to give us. Our level of dependence on another should grow slowly and only in correlation to the depth of our acquired trust.

Learn to do reality checks.
Once we become aware of what lenses we wear, and how they impact what we see and hear and how we interpret reality, we need to humbly accept the fact that sometimes

our lenses cause us to get things wrong. Sometimes we see, hear, and interpret things incorrectly. But we will never know this unless we check out what we are perceiving.

This is why it's so important to learn to do reality checks in our newly developing relationships. Doing a reality check involves paying attention to my body, becoming aware of when I'm feeling fearful, angry, or insecure, connecting it to whatever situation triggered those feelings, and asking the other person if my interpretation is correct.

When I sense they are agitated with me, I simply ask, "You seem agitated with me. Am I reading you right?" More often than I care to admit, my lenses are foggy. I accurately assessed that they are upset, but I got the reason wrong. It had nothing to do with me. If I'm accurate in my perception, then we can talk about it. What did I do to irritate them?

This step cannot be skipped if we want to grow in understanding and trusting another.

Make re-do's a regular habit.
We all know there is no such thing as a conflict-free relationship. If we want to develop trust and intimacy with others, we must be willing to navigate *a lot* of conflict. Learning to own our mistakes and to give and receive

forgiveness is essential. No relationship will go anywhere deep without these.

TBRI taught me the importance of a "re-do." It's a beautiful way of extending grace to another. When someone behaves with you in a hurtful way, instead of responding in kind, you can simply ask them if they would like to try to say what they want to say again. Or you can try to be playful and say, "Um, how about we do a re-do?" Being playful even in heated moments can diffuse things quickly.

You can also ask the other person for a chance to do a re-do yourself when you know you just blew it, like the times when the words barely left your mouth before you wished you could take them back. We've all been there. We all need to give and receive grace and forgiveness. Ask for a re-do.

A note of caution:
Sadly, there will be those in our lives who are not worthy of our trust no matter how much we want it to be so. We must acknowledge this painful truth. It's extremely important to know how to discern whether a person is trustworthy or not so we can protect ourselves from those who are not.

A good principle to follow is to "take the log out of our own eye first, so we can clearly see others" (Matthew

7:5). If we are still too raw in our own wounding, our ability to accurately assess whom we can trust will be compromised. This is why it is crucial to have enough self-awareness to be able to say, "I always seem to get myself in situations trusting those I shouldn't."

If this is you, find a counselor who can help you sort out your issues before you begin to pursue growing in relationship with others. If a counselor is not accessible, find the safest person you know and ask for their advice before diving into new relationships, especially romantic ones. Remember, trust needs to be earned. Not everyone can or should be trusted.

CHAPTER 6 MEDITATIONS

1. What areas of awareness do you need to grow in?
2. Do you have a rich emotional vocabulary beyond I'm mad or I'm sad?
3. Do you value the importance of your emotions and the emotions of others?
4. Is it difficult for you to talk about your emotions? Listen to others' emotions?
5. Practice doing Body Mapping and a Body Scan. Did you notice anything new?
6. Do you have recurring health problems that have no explanation or that don't get better?
7. Did you know your brain has a neurological "on-off" switch for being able to connect with others?
8. Are you aware when your relational Wi-Fi is off?
9. What do you need to do when it is "off" to help yourself calm down?
10. How good are you at using your voice? What obstacles make it difficult for you?
11. Are you comfortable with the idea of asking for a reality check? A "re-do"?
12. Do you think these practices will help you grow in your ability to trust others and develop more meaningful relationships? Why or why not?

CHAPTER 6 REFERENCES

1. *The Body Keeps the Score: Brain, Mind, and Body in the Healing of Trauma*, Bessel A. van der Kolk (2014)
2. *In an Unspoken Voice: How the Body Releases Trauma and Restores Goodness*, Peter A. Levine (2010)

CHAPTER 7

CONCLUSION: THE JOURNEY

In the end, the Lord designed us to be in community with both Him and all of humanity. But this cannot happen without trust. If we want to live a deeply satisfying life, we must learn what gets in the way of that and how to overcome it. Nevertheless, reality is that only the Lord provides perfect community for us and does so always. The rest of humanity will be there for us, as we will be there for them, imperfectly and inconsistently.

Knowing this, how do we proceed? As I look back on my own journey of growing in trust of the Lord and others, it seems a bit like wandering a winding path in a forest. I'm not sure what's around the next bend. I know there are some dark patches, snakes, and steep rocky descents. I have fallen a time or two. But the path also leads to openings of unimaginable beauty. An incredible field of wildflowers, a gorgeous lake, or an unexpected waterfall take my breath away.

With humanity, I've been wounded by others both intentionally and unintentionally. And I have wounded others in like manner. Through it all, I have purposefully pursued understanding myself and my brokenness, as well as healing. This has allowed me to see more clearly who I should trust and who I should not. It's allowed me to come to grips with my role in broken relationships. I'm learning to use my voice more effectively, to pay attention to what my body is telling me, and to take risks in making myself appropriately dependent on others. I'm daring to trust others. As a result, I've developed relationships with people that have blessed me in ways I could never have dreamed of. And when things don't go well, I'm learning to ask for a "re-do." I'm growing in being able to constructively navigate conflicts and repairs in relationships. Conflict really isn't the end of the world.

I understand that this is a journey that will continue for the rest of my life, and I'm OK with that. I know I'm made for relationships, so I'm going to continue to pursue growing in how to develop rich, trusting ones. As I do, I feel more whole and connected.

With the Lord, my winding path has a bit of a different nuance. Trusting Him always seems to come back to the same questions. Is He real? Is He good? My journey started with His Word. Even as a young girl, His Word rang true to me. I didn't always understand it, but what I did understand resonated as true about me, the world, and humanity. I had no problem accepting the fact that I was a sinner who needed a Savior.

The more I read about Jesus, the more I was able to trust in His goodness. I began to trust Him with my child-like needs, problems with friends and boyfriends, or helping me find my lost kitten. He met me in these needs, and I began to sense His still, small voice guiding me at various points. I was able to see Him working in my life.

The older I got, I needed to trust Him for more difficult things. Again, I wrestled with the questions, Is He real? Is He good? I was able to look back and remember the ways in which He had met me clearly already. This should have been enough. But I think we are all predisposed to doubt. Did it really happen the way I was remembering? Was I just making this up? Could He be trusted in this situation? And what about His Word? What about some of the doubts my professors cast on it?

To address my questions about the veracity of the Bible, I began to study various aspects of documentary criticism (a field of study on assessing if ancient documents are legitimate) as well as history, archaeology, fulfilled prophecies, and a little geology. Simultaneously, I was actively living the double life I discussed in the introduction.

The further I wandered from biblical guidance, the more consequences I reaped. Both in my study and my life, I became convinced that the Word of God was true. I had resolved the issue for myself that He was real. Then the questions became, Would I submit to the words of the Bible? To Him? There was more wrestling to do.

I had to make sense of the suffering I was seeing both near and far: friends being killed in car accidents or overdoses, rape, sexual abuse, poverty, domestic violence, witchcraft, etc. Where was God in all of this? How could He possibly be good? How could I trust Him? I had no answer to these questions. I only knew that His Word was true, He was real, I needed a Savior, and I couldn't manage my life on my own. I was desperate.

So, I decided to submit my life to Him and trust Him in the darkness. And He met me there. (See Chapter 4 for some of the insights He taught me.) I understand what the writer of Hebrews meant when he penned, "He who comes to God must believe that He is and that He is a rewarder of those who seek Him" (Hebrews 11:6).

Now, for any given situation where I'm struggling to trust the Lord, I start with His word. Are there any promises that are relevant? What biblical characters or passages give me instruction or encouragement in this? Then I ask myself which areas of His character I'm specifically having trouble trusting. Is it *His ability* or *His willingness* to provide for me? His protection? His love for me personally? His predictability? Then I remember the ways He has come through for me in the past, all the times He has provided for, protected, and sustained me and my family. Each memory is like a physical memorial or "Ebenezer stone" that I carry with me. I may have to repeat this process several times in a sitting until I reach a point of confidence and peace. For particularly difficult issues, I must repeat this process often throughout the day. It has helped me grow in my ability to be still and know that He is God, and to trust Him.

The journey has been full of twists and turns for sure. But I've learned that He is good, very good. His Word and His Spirit guide me. They comfort me when I'm confused or the path is dark. The more I trust Him and follow what He says, the more I see Him move in my life. I have increasing numbers of Ebenezer stones along my path that I can look to for evidence of His faithfulness and kindness to me and my family.

This gives me confidence to trust Him in the next situation. It has been an imperfect yet upward spiral of trust, evidence, and trusting more. And I affirm with David his words of Psalm 103. Yes! He has satisfied my years with good things.

My hope and prayer are that this book will encourage you to continue to pursue growth in trusting both God and worthy people, knowing that until the day we experience flawless community and harmony among all of creation in the realized Kingdom of God, we can still find sufficient comfort and rest in God alone. Alone we came from Him, and alone we will return to Him. His perfect love will cast out all our fear and anxiety if we fall into His arms and trust Him as we learn to love and trust others.

Melinda A. Cathey, M.A.
Co-Founder, The Harbor, St. Petersburg, Russia
Consultant/Educator for Trauma Informed Care

Melinda received her Master of Arts in Counseling Psychology in 1985 from Trinity Evangelical Divinity School. She practiced individual, family, and marriage counseling in a variety of settings, including community health, church, and private practice.

In 1992, Melinda and her husband, Mark, and the first of their three children moved to St. Petersburg, Russia, where they served as missionaries. In 2001, she cofounded The Harbor with Alex Krutov and served as its executive director until 2015. The Harbor was the first transitional care program of its kind in St. Petersburg and the second in Russia. Its distinctives include residential care, an individualized and holistic program, a focus on the psychological and spiritual aspects of development and trauma, and a commitment to professional and highly trained staff.

In 2015, Melinda completed TBRI (Trust Based Relational Intervention) Educator Training under the study of Dr. David Cross and the late Dr. Karyn Purvis, who co-founded the program at Texas Christian University in Fort Worth, Texas. Melinda trains and consults nationally and internationally on trauma-informed therapy and The Harbor model of residential care with those working with orphans or foster kids in any capacity. Her training of TBRI principles has been enthusiastically received in Russia, Ukraine, Mexico, Bolivia, Colombia, Honduras, Ecuador, Peru, and the United States.